Teachers Evaluating Teachers

SOCIAL PHILOSOPHY & POLICY CENTER

Teachers Evaluating Teachers

Peer Review and the New Unionism

by MYRON LIEBERMAN

transaction

Transaction Publishers
New Brunswick (USA) and London (UK)

Published by the Social Philosophy and Policy Center and by Transaction
Publishers 1998

Library of Congress Cataloging-in-Publication Data

Lieberman, Myron, 1919–
    Teachers evaluating teachers : peer review and the new unionism /
Myron Lieberman.
        p.   cm. — (Studies in social philosophy & policy ; no. 20)
    Includes bibliographical references and index.
    ISBN 1-56000-381-2 (cloth). — ISBN 0-7658-0461-1 (pbk.)
    1. Teachers—Rating of—United States.   2. Teachers—Rating of—
Ohio—Columbus.   3. Teachers—Rating of—Ohio—Toledo.   4. Peer
review—United States.   5. Peer review—Ohio—Columbus.   6. Peer
review—Ohio—Toledo.   7. Teachers' unions—United States.
I. Title.   II. Series.
LB2838.L54   1998
371.14′4′0973—dc21   98-13441
                                                                              CIP

Cover Design: Kathy Horn
Cover image copyright © 1998 PhotoDisc, Inc.

It is fairly evident that the individuals conspicuously active in urging extensive social changes are not generally those who are even relatively most competent in their judgment of social facts and values and the consequences of possible measures. Humility and modesty go with deep insight, and those who see farthest into the problems see their difficulty and are reticent about writing prescriptions even for admitted evils. (This is commonly interpreted as favouring the evils.)

And still less can the advocates of extensive reforms be regarded as disinterested. Almost in the nature of the case, they would be the agents to carry out the changes proposed, and to administer the new system if adopted; and their interest can hardly be unaffected by the realization of this fact. In short, advocacy of extensive reform is practically the solicitation of the position of king on the part of the reformer. And under competitive conditions the solicitation tends to take a form in which it will be effective in gaining power for the agitators, which does not mean clearness, and inclusive accuracy, regarding the changes to be brought about. The reformer typically has in fact little in the way of a definite programme, but preaches vague ideals in terms admitting of little dispute. In an age of experimental science, he also rather typically advocates experimental procedure—with himself as experimenter and society as experimented upon.

—Frank H. Knight, *The Ethics of Competition*

Series Editor: Ellen Frankel Paul
Series Managing Editor: Harry Dolan

The Social Philosophy and Policy Center, founded in 1981, is an interdisciplinary research institution whose principal mission is the examination of public policy issues from a philosophical perspective. In pursuit of this objective, the Center supports the work of scholars in the fields of political science, philosophy, law, and economics. In addition to this book series, the Center hosts scholarly conferences and edits an interdisciplinary professional journal, *Social Philosophy & Policy*. For further information on the Center, write to: Social Philosophy and Policy Center, Bowling Green State University, Bowling Green, OH 43403.

Contents

Acknowledgments

I would like to thank Fieldstead & Company and the William H. Donner Foundation for their early assistance on matters that culminated in this book. As always, I am grateful to the Social Philosophy and Policy Center, Bowling Green State University, Ohio, which provided the editorial and other support that made it possible to complete the research and publish the results.

1

Introduction: Why This Book?

Since the publication of *A Nation at Risk* in 1983,[1] educational reform has become a mini-industry in the United States. Diagnoses of our educational ailments, real or alleged, have identified scores of factors deemed responsible for our nation's educational shortcomings: poverty, federal control of education, family breakdown, drug abuse, television, the sexual revolution, racial and gender discrimination, group preferences, the decline of community, low teacher pay—the list goes on and on. It is only in recent years, however, that public opinion has seriously considered the possibility that the National Education Association (NEA) and the American Federation of Teachers (AFT) are obstacles to reform. Clearly, the teacher unions themselves are aware of this changing attitude and are doing their utmost to counteract it. After decades of denial, the NEA and the AFT concede that the unions have had a negative impact upon certain school operations. The criticism most often conceded by the unions is their tendency to render it extremely difficult for school districts to fire incompetent teachers. (For editorial simplicity, I shall also include teachers guilty of egregious moral conduct as "incompetent.")

For present purposes, the point is that the NEA and the AFT claim to be forging a "new union" partly as a response to criticisms of their excessive zeal in defending incompetent teachers. The "new union" (or "new unionism") is not a clearly defined program or change in the NEA/AFT governance structure. Instead, it is supposedly a change in the role of the teacher unions, especially with respect to teachers who are performing poorly. This is especially evident from

1

statements by NEA president Robert F. Chase at the National Press Club in 1997 and 1998. Speaking as a "Morning Newsmaker" on February 11, 1998, Chase told the assembled reporters: "Yet many questions remain about what exactly 'new unionism' is, and where it's going. I cannot provide a map or a manifesto—because I'm not writing the script. The fact is, National Education Association members are writing it together." Chase then described "new unionism as it is emerging—a new unionism not of theory, but of nuts-and-bolts practice in hundreds, if not thousands, of NEA affiliates."[2]

In my opinion, Chase's statement simply lists a few alleged good deeds by NEA affiliates without in any way clarifying the distinguishing features of the "new unionism."[3] It appears, however, that "new unions" collaborate with management, exercise responsibility for student achievement, and are "risk takers"—without clarification of what the risks are, and who bears what consequences if the risks turn out badly. As Chase himself points out, NEA affiliates were acting in the "new union" mode before it was characterized as such—all of which adds to uncertainty over whether the phrase refers to something new, or is simply a "snappy name" for what NEA affiliates already do, or claim to be doing.

In any case, the new unionism does not accept all the criticisms directed at the teacher unions; it is a reaction only to the criticisms that the unions acknowledge have some merit. In the following analysis, the basic issue is whether the new unionism will minimize the entry and/or retention of incompetent teachers. This issue is very important, not only in its own right but as a test of NEA/AFT willingness to subordinate union interests to broader ones. The analysis does not consider most of the criticisms that the NEA and the AFT ignore or explicitly reject. Inasmuch as the unions themselves concede that they have been insufficiently concerned about incompetent teachers, their proposals to deal with the issue should be a good test of the new unionism.

In this context, "peer review" is the most prominent feature of the new unionism and the one accorded the most attention here. The NEA is by far the larger of the two unions, and has done more to articulate the idea of a "new union" or the imperative need to "reinvent the union." Perhaps the most prominent NEA statement on the topic was Robert Chase's National Press Club address in February 1997; in his presentation, later disseminated broadly to NEA members and the media, Chase asserted that educational quality would now be the highest NEA priority.[4] The primary means for effectuating this new priority was to be "peer review." Although it has not been defined precisely, "peer review" is widely understood to encompass various procedures by which teachers and their unions would exercise more responsibility for improving teacher performance as well as for terminating the services of teachers who do not perform adequately after receiving assistance.

Under Chase's leadership, the NEA's 1997 Representative Assembly adopted Resolution New D-6, "Peer Assistance and Review Programs" (see Appendix A). This resolution cleared the way for NEA's state and local affiliates to adopt peer review plans that did not jeopardize any benefits or support available from the NEA. Prior to the adoption of New D-6, the NEA would not support or defend teachers who participated in peer review plans as "consulting teachers," the phrase most commonly used to denote teachers who assist and/or evaluate other teachers in peer review plans. New D-6, therefore, constituted a break from the NEA's previous policy of not supporting its members when they were acting in a supervisory capacity; the resolution immediately became the focal point in the ongoing NEA effort to be perceived as the leader of the education-reform movement.

The adoption of New D-6 was preceded by an NEA-sponsored study that characterized reform leadership as essential to the survival of public education, and hence to the NEA's role as the leading partner in the public-education coalition.[5] It would be belaboring the obvious to cite other evidence that within the NEA, there is widespread acknowledgment that both public education and the association are in disrepute and that something must be done about it. That "something" is the new unionism that is discussed here.

The AFT has not emphasized the phrase "new union," but like the NEA, it has emphasized the importance of reordering union priorities to accord greater weight to educational achievement. With respect to both unions, however, the question is whether their underlying concern is over the substance or the appearance of reform leadership. A related issue already being discussed in both unions is whether the new unionism can be reconciled with core union functions. Of course, the answer depends on what changes in union philosophy and practice are forthcoming as a result of the new unionism. Inasmuch as the unions, especially the NEA, point to peer review as the most significant feature of the new unionism, analysis of it should be a useful guide to the significance of the new unionism.

Peer review is utilized for three different purposes. First, it is a procedure culminating in decisions to renew or not renew the contracts of first-year teachers. Peer review is also a procedure leading up to decisions about tenured teachers who are not performing adequately for one reason or another. A third purpose is to provide assistance to teachers without any implication of adverse action; a teacher wants help and peer review is the process used to provide it. As we shall see, these differences are very important, legally and practically. When a school district is said to be using peer review, it is essential to specify the purpose(s) for which it is utilized. Otherwise, the conclusions reached are likely to be applied erroneously to other modes of peer review.

The analysis proceeds as follows. Chapter 2 is devoted to peer review in operation. In practice, the "peers" are usually designated as "consulting teachers" and that is how they are designated here. Peer review plans do or can differ with respect to the manner in which consulting teachers are chosen, their responsibilities, the number of new teachers per consulting teacher, the compensation of consulting teachers, the role of principals, and so forth. Therefore, analysis of peer review plans must take their actual or potential differences into account; otherwise, comments that apply to peer review generally may not be valid when applied to particular plans. Chapter 2 also discusses the role of peer review as it affects tenured teachers and peer review as assistance to teachers who want help apart from any threat of adverse action for failure to improve.

As will be evident, peer review presents a number of challenges to conventional union/management relations, especially to the role of principals. These challenges are analyzed in Chapter 3. Chapter 4 is devoted to the claim that peer review is a major step toward the professionalization of teachers; under peer review, teachers are supposed to accept collective responsibility for teacher competence. The discussion shows that the claim is based upon a widespread confusion between employment and professional decisions. Chapter 5 continues the discussion by showing how unions that adopt peer review try to meet their obligation to provide due process for teachers who face termination. Chapter 6 examines the costs of peer review, a critical but widely neglected issue in media and professional discussions of the topic.

Both the NEA and the AFT have cited union/management relations at the General Motors Saturn plant in Spring Hill, Tennessee, as a desirable model for union/management relations in education; for this reason, Chapter 7 reviews labor/management relations at the Saturn plant to assess their feasibility in public education. Rather surprisingly, the NEA and the AFT have promoted peer review without much attention to its prevalence in higher education. Chapter 7 points out the similarities and dissimilarities between peer review in K–12 and higher education. The major conclusion is that the basic arguments for and against peer review are the same in both sectors.

Chapter 8 is an effort to shed some light on the union stake in peer review. Unlike analyses that assume that the unions support peer review on educational grounds, Chapter 8 shows that the unions have strong reason to promote peer review for union and teacher welfare reasons.

Chapter 9 then summarizes the positive and negative features of peer review. The conclusion is that its potential is vastly overrated and that it is likely to create a host of problems in the unions and school districts that establish such programs. The alleged success of peer review programs in a handful of school districts is attributed to a failure to raise important issues, such as the costs of peer review, and to a reliance upon assumptions instead of credible evidence to demonstrate "success," however the term is defined.

As important as it may be, peer review is only one dimension of the new unionism. Chapter 10, therefore, spells out some features of the new unionism that is needed if the unions are to play a positive role in promoting teacher quality as well as teacher welfare. Of course, many observers believe that no union of any kind is necessary or even desirable. I do not agree, but perhaps the term "union" is the problem. A wealth of experience tells us that individuals are usually helpless to oppose arbitrary government. Perhaps a truly competitive market system would provide the needed protections, but although there is considerable support for movement in that direction, it will not eliminate the need or desirability of teacher organizations, whether or not they are labeled "unions." Consequently, Chapter 10 summarizes the characteristics of a "new unionism" that would facilitate higher levels of educational achievement at lower costs.

Despite the publicity accorded to peer review in the past few years, very few school districts have actually adopted peer review programs. For this reason, the discussion relies heavily on peer review programs in a few school districts such as those in Columbus and Toledo, Ohio, which operate the most widely praised and publicized programs in the nation. Although both plans include an intervention procedure for tenured teachers, most of their resources are devoted to assisting and evaluating new teachers, the topic that receives most of the attention in this book.

The Toledo peer review program was conceived in the 1970s and initiated in 1981. Although the program was initiated by the Toledo Federation of Teachers (TFT), an AFT affiliate, the National Education Association (NEA) has also praised and utilized the Toledo plan as a guide in working with NEA affiliates interested in peer review. Of course, conclusions about the success or failure of peer review should not depend solely on its operation in a few school districts, especially when all the elements of peer review might vary from school district to school district. Nevertheless, on many issues, the Columbus and Toledo plans are a useful point of departure, since they are widely and favorably publicized by both unions.

A Note on Peer Review and Collective Bargaining

The new unionism proposes to utilize collective bargaining as the vehicle for initiating and implementing educational reforms such as peer review. For this reason, it is essential to understand the relationships between peer review and collective bargaining. The issue is not whether collective bargaining does or does not affect educational reform, but how it does so and what are the limits, if any, to collective bargaining as the vehicle of reform.

The main rationale for collective bargaining as the vehicle for school reform emphasizes the constant turnover among school management, especially in large urban districts. The idea is that collective bargaining contracts can mitigate the negative consequences of this turnover by codifying desirable reforms, thereby providing the continuity essential to their effectiveness. This rationale overlooks the fact, or at least the possibility, that the constant turnover is the result of public dissatisfaction and that the public must retain the right to change policies and remove policymakers when it is dissatisfied with them; policies incorporated in union contracts constitute a limitation on the public's ability to change policies that it no longer wishes to support. Indeed, this rationale for collective bargaining suggests a basic conflict between public-sector bargaining and democratic representative government.

Significantly, peer review has not emerged outside of states and school districts in which teachers bargain collectively. One reason is that peer review has been a union initiative, and NEA/AFT affiliates have more leverage in states and districts that have authorized teachers to bargain collectively. Another reason is that school management must assume certain contractual obligations as part of a peer review plan. It is very difficult if not practically impossible to require management to fulfill these obligations outside of collective bargaining situations.

Although collective bargaining makes peer review possible, it also poses some major legal and practical problems in implementing peer review. For example, the teacher unions, like other unions, bargain over "terms and conditions of employment." Despite some legal uncertainties about what this covers, and variations in the state bargaining laws, some features of peer review ostensibly conflict with collective bargaining statutes. For example, according to most of the bargaining statutes, the unions cannot require school management to bargain over terms and conditions of employment for school personnel performing supervisory duties. Because peer review requires some teachers, often referred to as "consulting teachers," to perform such duties, it typically involves bargaining on this topic. The conflict is resolved in different ways in different states and school districts. Changing the bargaining law is one solution. Changing the peer review program is another, as is dropping the effort to introduce peer review.

The following chapters devote considerable attention to the relationships between collective bargaining and peer review. In doing so, it is hardly possible to overemphasize the importance of the specific state statutes that affect the issue. Any failure to take these statutes into account is likely to result in erroneous conclusions about these relationships.

Differences among Peer Review Programs

As emphasized at the outset, peer review plans differ in several ways. For example, in Rochester, New York, the "lead teachers" (the equivalent of "consulting teachers" in Toledo) are appointed for two years but can be reappointed;

in 1997, sixty-three out of 123 lead teachers had previously served in this role. In contrast, consulting teachers in Toledo are appointed for three-year nonrenewable terms. The Career in Teaching Panel, the governing body of Rochester's peer review program, consists of four teachers and four administrators; in Toledo, the governing board consists of five teachers appointed by the union and four designated management representatives. Teachers in Rochester become eligible to serve as lead teachers in their eighth year of service, compared to five in Columbus, and their applications must meet a somewhat different set of requirements. And so forth.

With respect to all such differences, the issue is whether they reflect a critical difference or are minor details that should not affect assessment of the peer review program. The differences must be analyzed on a case-by-case basis, and obviously there will be disagreements about their importance. Similar issues arise with respect to the applicability of private-sector initiatives intended to establish a new unionism. Teacher unions are not the only unions that are rethinking their role in the workplace and in society. On the contrary, several large national unions have been forced to reconsider their roles and responsibilities in recent years. This development also characterizes unions in other Western industrial nations; to some extent, the reasons apply to private-sector unions regardless of country. For instance, the international mobility of capital and the power of private-sector employers to shift production to other countries is a major union problem that cuts across nations and industries, especially when the industry relies heavily on operations that utilize low-skilled and low-wage workers. This particular issue does not directly affect teacher unions; school boards cannot shift their operations to contiguous communities, let alone to other countries. Although the NEA and the AFT oppose the North American Free Trade Agreement (NAFTA) and fast-track authority to negotiate trade agreements, they do so only to accommodate their allies in organized labor. Indeed, it can be (and is) argued that the teacher unions are acting against the interests of their members by adopting protectionist positions on trade issues.

Nevertheless, many factors that have stimulated interest in the "new unionism" in the private sector are applicable to teacher unions. Some of these crosscutting factors are as follows:

1. Unions in the United States are based upon legal approval and enactment of exclusive representation. Under exclusive representation, one union has the sole authority to negotiate terms and conditions of employment for all the employees in an appropriate bargaining unit, whether or not they are union members. Although universally established in both the public and private sectors in the United States, exclusive representation is not the practice in many democratic nations and is being criticized on several grounds in the U.S.

2. The union movement in the U.S. emerged as a reaction to what was perceived to be the excessive power of the employers over individual employees. Strong unions were deemed essential to counteract the employers' power, but strong unions tend to be unions that minimize internal dissent, often by coercive means. There is some thought that U.S. unions have gone much too far in stifling internal dissent to maximize their bargaining power.

3. Since the 1960s, a plethora of federal and state laws have expanded the rights of individual employees. These rights do not depend on union intervention. For instance, various statutes protect employees individually against discrimination on the basis of race, sex, age, and/or disability. In some cases, the expansion of these individual rights has led to conflict within unions; for example, employees asserting racial discrimination sometimes find themselves in conflict with unions committed to seniority as a guiding principle of union policy. In many situations, the complaining parties utilize representation by nonunion sources, such as civil rights organizations, broadly defined. These situations give rise to concern over the appropriate role for unions in enforcing the statutory rights of employees.

4. A variety of polls, many sponsored by the unions themselves, reveal widespread disinterest in unionization, even among workers who can be considered strong potential supporters of it. Moreover, public opinion polls show widespread public concern about union activities. Substantial segments of our population are less likely to support a candidate for public office if the candidate is supported by labor unions.[6] Paradoxically, the NEA is viewed more favorably than most other unions because many citizens do not think of the NEA as a union.

The preceding factors are by no means exhaustive, but they may help to explain the interest in the new unionism. Needless to say, there is much disagreement within organized labor, as well as among academics and employer representatives, about what the new unionism is or will be or should be. There is a wealth of literature on the topic; unfortunately, most of it is irrelevant to public-sector unions. One reason may be the dramatically different public- and private-sector patterns of union density, that is, the percentage of the labor force that is unionized. While private-sector unionization has declined from 36 percent of the private-sector labor force in 1953 to less than 11 percent in 1997, union density in the public sector has experienced phenomenal increases at every level of government. The NEA and the AFT illustrate this point. NEA membership increased from 765,000 in 1961–62 to 2,300,000 in 1997–98; AFT membership went from 60,700 to 947,000 during the same period. Although the 1997–98 figures include large numbers of retirees, support personnel, and student members, there is no doubt that regular teacher membership has increased dramatically. Nonetheless, both the NEA and the AFT agree that public education is in danger of losing the support of the American people; if this loss of confidence is not reversed or at least halted, the teacher unions will decline along with their private-sector counterparts.

In the context of organized labor, peer review is an anomaly. The concerns that give rise to it are present in private-sector as well as public-sector unions; however, because teachers are public employees, peer review in public education encounters problems that are absent in the private sector. This issue comes to the fore whenever the discussion considers the new unionism in public education.

2

Peer Review in Operation

The purpose of this chapter is to describe how peer review functions. For the reasons previously mentioned, the discussion will feature the Columbus and Toledo programs while recognizing that others may differ in important respects.[1]

The Toledo program was first proposed in the 1970s and was implemented in September 1981. The driving force behind the program was Dal Lawrence, president of the Toledo Federation of Teachers (TFT) for thirty years until his retirement in 1997, when he was succeeded in the office by his wife, Francine Lawrence. The governing body of the Toledo program is a nine-member Board of Review. The board is responsible for selecting and monitoring the work of the consulting teachers; the latter assist and evaluate first-year teachers ("interns") and tenured teachers who have been notified that their teaching is or may be unsatisfactory for one reason or another. The board is also responsible for recommending to the Superintendent of Schools the future employment status of teachers subject to peer review. Consulting teachers are appointed for three-year terms that are not renewable except in unusual circumstances.

As I have noted, the Board of Review consists of nine members. Five are appointed by the union; the other four are the administrators who hold the following positions: Assistant Superintendent for Human Resources, Deputy Director for Human Resources, Executive Director for High Schools, and Executive Director for Elementary Schools. The chairmanship of the Board of

Review is rotated annually between the TFT president and the Assistant Superintendent for Human Resources, who serves as the chairman of the administrative team. Six votes are required for a Board of Review action; it appears, however, that from 1981 to 1997 there was not a single instance of a complete split between the administration and union appointees to the board.[2]

The board's main functions are to choose and monitor the work of the consulting teachers, and to recommend the future employment status of the interns to the Superintendent of Schools. The board also recommends what action is to be taken with respect to tenured teachers who are subject to intervention. Although the Superintendent of Schools then makes his own recommendations to the board of education, no superintendent had rejected a recommendation of the Board of Review as of the fall of 1997.[3]

The Consulting Teachers

The consulting teachers are recruited from the ranks of Toledo's regular teaching staff. Applicants must complete an application form and submit recommendations attesting to the quality of their teaching from (1) their building representative (that is, a teacher who acts as a union representative for a particular school); (2) their principal; and (3) three other teachers in their school. Obviously, this requirement raises some important issues, such as the prospects for outstanding teachers who are not union members or are opposed to the union leadership. Inasmuch as only twenty-three out of 2,500 teachers are not members of the TFT, federation leaders do not regard this as a significant problem; however, the possibility that many teachers join the TFT only because they would have to pay the dues anyway cannot be dismissed so easily. Furthermore, members have only a narrow window period in which to resign; hence, teachers who joined voluntarily are not necessarily voluntary members later on. The consulting teachers are appointed by the co-chairs of the Board of Review for a three-year nonrenewable term; in effect, this means that the administration and the union each have a veto power over candidates. Some candidates have attained the rank of "master teacher" in the Toledo Career Ladder program, but all are subject to an interview process and unannounced observations of their teaching by board representatives.

Insofar as possible, the selection and assignment of consulting teachers is arranged so that they serve with interns who teach the same subject and/or grade level. When this is not possible, it may be necessary to bring in an expert in the subject matter or reappoint a consulting teacher after his or her three-year term. Obviously, the smaller the school district in terms of the number of teachers, the more difficult it will be to restrict consulting teachers to a three-year term without renewal.

Once the TFT has determined the required number of consulting teachers and their teaching fields, the federation advertises for applications. Although some positions can be filled long before school opens, the final complement of consulting teachers is not known until a few days before school opens in the fall. Usually there is a small excess of approved candidates over vacancies, so that approved candidates are usually selected as consulting teachers within two years after approval.

Applicants approved by the Assistant Superintendent for Human Resources and the TFT president are subjected to unscheduled observations that are summarized for the Board of Review. If the report is favorable, the applicant is placed in the pool of consulting teachers and begins attending Board of Review meetings. A few applicants have complained about their exclusion from the pool, but they have no practical redress on the issue. Teachers aspiring to be principals are discouraged from applying, but a substantial minority of consulting teachers participate in Toledo's Career Ladder program. This program, administered jointly by the school district and the TFT, requires participants to demonstrate a higher level of professional competence than is needed to remain in good standing and receive the regular increments on the salary schedule. The union regards the Career Ladder program as a system of merit pay based on peer review.

The Toledo and Columbus programs differ in the training programs for consulting teachers. In Toledo, the consulting teachers receive only a two-day training program before beginning their classroom observations and meetings with interns. The rationale for this extremely brief period of training is that the consulting teachers receive additional training as a result of their meetings with other consulting teachers, including those who are in their second or third year in this role.

In Columbus, the consulting teachers receive training, mainly through university courses, for a year before they work as consulting teachers. During their first year of service as consulting teachers, they receive additional training at a workshop every other Friday afternoon. In general, however, the training in Columbus takes place in the evening. Significantly, the consulting teachers do not pay for the training courses but receive credit on the salary schedule for them; in effect, then, they are paid to take them.

In both Columbus and Toledo, consulting teachers are relieved of their regular teaching duties so that they can devote their time to assisting interns. The average load of consulting teachers in Toledo is nine interns, fewer if the consultant is also responsible for a teacher in the intervention program. The consulting teacher spends about a half a day each week with each intern, more if the intern is experiencing major problems. In contrast, the consulting teacher workload in Columbus is eighteen interns, or fifteen in addition to one intervention case.

In 1997–98, the consulting teachers in Toledo were paid $5,000 above their regular salary. They were also paid for any extracurricular assignment they may have had, even though they do not perform the assignment while serving as consulting teachers. Data on compensation for extracurricular assignments not performed were not available, but except for master teachers in the Career Ladder program (who are not paid an additional stipend for service as consulting teachers), compensation as a consulting teacher is a major benefit to Toledo teachers. In Columbus, the consulting teachers are paid 20 percent above the salary for beginning teachers, but compensation for extracurricular assignments is not included. In 1997–98, the salary for first-year teachers in Columbus was $29,403; hence, consulting teachers were paid $5,881 above their regular salary.

The Columbus and Toledo plans differ with respect to their treatment of the interns. In Toledo, the interns pay only half of the regular federation dues. The rationale is that except for union support in case of contract termination or nonrenewal, the interns are entitled to all of the rights and privileges of regular teachers. In contrast, the Columbus interns are charged full dues and receive union support in case the intern challenges nonrenewal. In both unions, the intern responses to the program have been substantially positive.

The Work of Consulting Teachers

The consulting teachers observe and confer with interns frequently and are required to submit timely reports on forms approved by the school district and the union. Prior to service, the consulting teachers in Toledo undergo a two-day training program. Union officials assert that frequent interaction between new and experienced consulting teachers during the school year obviates the need for extended formal training prior to service as a consulting teacher. Be that as it may, the 1997–98 budget for the Ohio State Department of Education includes funds for training on peer review, with Columbus and Toledo personnel in the leadership roles.

Although they are accorded wide latitude in how to assist interns, the consulting teachers are required to track the interns' progress in four categories:

(1) Teaching procedures
(2) Classroom management
(3) Knowledge of subject matter
(4) Personal characteristics and professional responsibilities

Each of these broad performance criteria is broken down into specific goals for the intern and supportive activities by the consulting teachers (see Appendix B). The consulting teachers are required to submit evaluations by December 20 and March 20 of each school year, with copies of all supporting documents. The March 20 evaluation reports also include the consulting teachers' recommendations on the future employment status of the interns. Inasmuch as some interns may be continued in this status after the first year, the consulting teachers must choose one of the following reemployment options:

- Recommended for first one-year contract
- Recommended for second one-year contract
- Recommended for initial four-year contract
- Recommended for third one-year contract
- Not recommended for reappointment

As Appendix E shows, the principals are responsible only for evaluating the interns on professional responsibilities; these relate primarily to the interns' respect for and adherence to school policies and regulations. *"Principals do not observe the classroom performance of interns nor evaluate same;* however, they are required to review their observations and evaluations on other matters with the interns and the consulting teachers, so that the latter can reinforce any recommendations for improvement made by the principals."[4]

Three formal observations are the minimum required during the intern year; a "formal observation" is defined as one that lasts at least twenty uninterrupted minutes and is followed by a conference with the intern within five days. The Teacher Summary Evaluation Report (Appendix C) is used as the basis for the required observations and conferences. Any negative recommendation relating to reemployment must be based on at least two observations, spaced over several months. In practice, the consulting teachers average about five observations per intern per semester.

If an intern is reemployed, responsibility for observations and evaluations thereafter falls solely on his or her principal. Two observations at a minimum are required during the second year. The same evaluation forms are used in both the first and second years to ensure continuity and consistency among evaluators. A second-year teacher can request a formal evaluation by a consulting teacher, and any such evaluation is accorded equal value with any other evaluation in appraising the teacher's performance. Consulting teachers are provided released time to conduct the evaluations of second-year teachers but are not allowed to consult with any administrator prior to their observation and conference with the second-year teacher. Optional peer evaluation in the second year appears to be an opportunity to rebut negative evaluations by principals, but the option is seldom exercised by second-year teachers. Probationary teachers in their second year may be required to serve a third probationary year, but if they are evaluated by the same principal as in the second year, they must be dismissed or awarded a four-year contract at the conclusion of the third year.

The principals' evaluations of the second-year teachers are sent to the Office of Human Resources, which makes all recommendations to the superintendent on the reemployment of probationary teachers, except those pertaining to first-year teachers. Essentially, the evaluation of new teachers is a two-stage process, with peer review playing the dominant role during the first year and the administration taking over the process in the second year. At all stages, the probationary teachers must be shown their evaluations and accorded an opportunity to respond to them.

What has been the impact of peer review on the reemployment of interns? From 1981–82 through 1996–97, 2,004 teachers were placed in the intern program. The outcomes over this period were as follows: of the 2,004 teachers in the program, sixty-eight were not renewed ("not renewed" means that the teacher was not offered reemployment for reasons other than poor performance), twelve were terminated, eighty resigned (resignations do not include transfers out of the district), and 1,844 were offered reemployment. Thus, 92 percent were offered reemployment.[5]

As will be evident, Toledo spends a great deal on observing, guiding, and evaluating first-year teachers; unfortunately, it is impossible to compare the relevant conditions and results under peer review with the previous situation in the district.

Intervention in Toledo

Intervention is a process whereby the school district and the union try to assist experienced teachers who have been identified as having to improve or be terminated. Clearly, the union's role in intervention is much more controversial within the union than any other mode of peer review; unions that adopt peer review for interns do not necessarily adopt it for tenured teachers, especially if the consulting teachers and the union would be involved in recommendations to terminate tenured teachers.

Toledo is one of the few districts in which the union plays a major role in recommendations to dismiss tenured teachers. In Toledo, both the principal and the union's building representative must agree to invoke intervention or it does not take place. Subsequently, the Board of Review, on which the union has a majority, must also approve the intervention. In effect, this gives the union a veto power over removal of incompetent tenured teachers. Obviously, giving a private organization such power over the employment status of public employees raises some troublesome public policy issues; it is hardly surprising that the school district tried to weaken union control over teacher evaluation in the 1997 and 1998 negotiations between the parties.

The steps in intervention are as follows:

(1) The principal consults with the Office of Human Resources, and the TFT building representative consults with the TFT president regarding the possible intervention.

(2) If authorized to proceed, the principal and the building representative meet to discuss the matter.

(3) A meeting is held with the entire union building committee to explain the need for intervention.

(4) The building committee and the principal interview the teacher about the possible intervention. After the interview, the building committee votes by secret ballot. If the vote is to initiate intervention, and the principal agrees, the principal and the building representative complete a Teacher Intervention Form (see Appendix D) and send it to the Office of Human Resources and the TFT.

(5) The principal and the building representative meet with the teacher affected to deliver and explain the notice of intervention. The teacher has the right to appeal the decision to an impartial arbitrator.

(6) If the arbitrator sustains the rationale for intervention and the procedures utilized to invoke it, a consulting teacher is assigned by the co-chairs of the Board of Review.

(7) The consulting teacher meets with the building representative and the principal to discuss:
   • the purpose of the intervention
   • the role of the intervener
   • the kinds of help that might be offered
   • the length of the intervention and the purpose of the status report to be prepared by the consulting teacher

(8) The consulting teacher works with the teacher affected to bring about improvement.

(9) Because the situations leading to intervention are so different, there is no prescribed procedure for how the intervention is carried out. At the conclusion of the intervention, the consulting teacher reviews the entire situation, including the kinds of assistance offered, with the principal and the building representative.

(10) The consulting teacher submits a status report to the Office of Human Resources and to the TFT. The form used depends on the contract status of the teacher who is the subject of the intervention, but includes the consulting teacher's conclusions as to whether the affected teacher is performing in a satisfactory manner.

(11) The Office of Human Resources then makes a recommendation to the superintendent on the future employment status of the teacher subject to intervention.

Table 2.1 shows that intervention has been invoked only forty-four times in the first twelve years of the peer review program.

There is some ambiguity among the categories in Table 2.1; for instance, some teachers may have resigned or retired rather than face termination proceedings. Regardless, the number of teachers involved in intervention, out of a total teaching force of approximately 2,500, was minuscule, especially in view of the fact that a much larger number of teachers were employed by the district over the twelve-year period. In view of the extended nature of many intervention cases, it is altogether possible that intervention delayed instead of facilitated the removal of incompetent teachers from Toledo classrooms. Furthermore, there is no data on such critical issues as the costs of intervention compared to the costs of conventional procedures.

Virtually every phase of peer review is affected by whether probationary or tenured teachers are involved. When probationary teachers are involved, the requirements for nonrenewal are typically not as rigorous; the criteria for not hiring a teacher are not as demanding as the criteria for terminating an experienced one. Where, as in Toledo, the criteria are the same, it is not likely that the criteria are applied with equal rigor. Furthermore, the unions can accommodate peer review of new teachers much more easily than peer review of tenured teachers who are in trouble for one reason or another. In the latter situation, the teacher's expectation of union support is much greater, and failure to provide it poses serious policy and legal problems for the unions. After all, it is one thing for first-year teachers not to receive union support; it is a much different matter when teachers who have paid union dues for ten or twenty years do not get union support when they need it most. Also, new teachers are not likely to be as influential as tenured teachers in the union. To be candid

Table 2.1.   Intervention Outcomes, Toledo, 1981–82 to 1992–93[6]

Number of Interventions	Outcomes
12	Satisfactorily completed intervention program
9	Retired
7	Resigned
7	Terminated
4	Disability retirement
2	Carried over
1	Death
1	Transfer to nonteaching
1	Continuous building substitute
44	Total interventions

and consistent, the unions would have to inform teachers that their annual dues do not buy union representation but only union assurance that the termination procedure will provide due process, with the teachers being left to support their cause from personal resources. Inasmuch as tenured teachers already enjoy due process as a matter of law, the assurance of due process under peer review may not be as attractive as the assurance of union representation in the absence of peer review.

Peer Review and Rank-and-File Teachers

The implications of peer review for tenured teachers should not be overlooked. In Toledo, more than 1,100 tenured teachers out of a total staff of about 2,500 are never evaluated, unless some complaint is made; in 1997, some had not been evaluated since 1970. Understandably, the Toledo school administration tried to make it possible to evaluate tenured teachers in its 1997 negotiations with the TFT. The district's position was supported by the *Toledo Blade* and the Parents Alliance for Children and Education (PACE), a local parents' group characterized by TFT leaders as the creation of the superintendent. Under Ohio law, when negotiations are at an impasse (that is, when further negotiations on any issue seem to be futile), the dispute is referred to a fact finder. The fact finder considers arguments presented by both parties to the dispute and then submits a report which is made public if the parties do not reach agreement on it or resolve their dispute in some other way. The controversy over teacher evaluation (or the lack thereof) was one of the three major issues submitted to a fact finder in the course of the TFT's contract dispute with the school district; the fact finder submitted a report on December 16, 1997, essentially supporting the district's position.

Intervention in Columbus

Peer review in Columbus is part of the district's Peer Assistance and Review Program (PAR Program), adopted in 1986. As in Toledo, intervention in Columbus requires approval by the PAR Panel, the governing body of the entire PAR Program. A unique feature of both programs is their dual track for experienced teachers for whom improvement is imperative. For example, the Columbus district has negotiated a set of procedures governing assistance to such teachers; the procedures vary according to the length of a teacher's service. Teachers needing improvement are sent a Notice of Special Evaluation which specifies the areas of unsatisfactory conduct and requires at least two observations of at least thirty minutes each by an administrator; however, any teacher with five years of continuous service in Columbus who has received a Notice of Special Evaluation must, upon request, be admitted to the PAR Program. Paragraph 401.14 of the union contract in Columbus reads as follows:

> Any teacher may request to be assigned to the PAR Program by submitting a written request to the Association President. If the teacher requesting assignment to the PAR Program has been given a Notice of Special Evaluation and has more than five (5) years of continuous Columbus teaching experience, such teacher shall be accepted into the intervention phase of the PAR Program. The final determination of whether to admit a teacher with five (5) or less years of continuous Columbus teaching experience to the PAR Program will be made by the PAR Panel.

Section 401.14 of the contract provides that during the time such a teacher is in the PAR Program, the evaluation and any related actions "shall be in accordance with the procedures established by the Peer Assistance and Review Program (PAR Program) rather than in accordance with the provisions of this Article 401." Note that the intervention procedures in Columbus and Toledo have no time limits. In Columbus, one intervention required three and a half years; in Toledo, the range was a few weeks to two and a half years, with one year as the most frequent duration. In view of the extended nature of the process, one must question whether its primary effect is to facilitate or to delay the removal of incompetent teachers.

Peer Review as "Assistance"

One way to structure the relationship between interns and consulting teachers would be for the latter to avoid evaluating interns. This option was emphasized in the 1997 NEA Representative Assembly debate over peer review. Peer review to *assist* teachers received much more support than peer review to *evaluate* teachers. However, if peer review is merely a device for "assisting" teachers, it cannot be legitimately characterized as a way for teachers to assume collective responsibility for the competence of teachers.

The peer review program in Toledo includes a School Consultation Program, cosponsored by the Toledo Board of Education and the TFT. Teachers can call for assistance on any matter of professional concern. The consultations are confidential and do not play any role in employment decisions. The program is utilized infrequently, but raises some interesting issues.

If "assistance" is the issue, what is the best way to provide it? There is no reason to assume that teachers released from class with pay are necessarily a more cost-effective way to assist teachers than observations and assistance by principals. Indeed, there are cogent reasons why peer review is probably a less cost-effective way to help teachers. First, peer review may be much more expensive than conventional procedures when all the costs are factored in. Second, we normally expect principals to be better qualified to help teachers since such help is part of the training and regular duties of principals. In contrast, consulting teachers are required to undertake only two days training prior to service in this capacity and are likely to serve as evaluators only on an ad hoc basis. In any event, if a school district wants to release teachers to assist other teachers, it is quite a stretch to characterize its actions as a step toward teacher professionalism and accountability.

Despite the overblown rhetoric, we can expect many local unions to press for peer review as assistance; many do so already as "mentoring," not "peer review" programs. In this mode, there is no actual or potential loss of union members. Consulting teachers get time off with pay for easier work; there is no accountability for results; and the process can be cited as rebutting the criticisms that the unions are not concerned about teacher quality. In short, peer review as assistance or as "mentoring" is simply a question of the best use of resources to assist and evaluate teachers without raising any labor/management or professional issues.

The Outcomes of Peer Review

Over the eleven-year period from 1986–87 to 1996–97, 3,312 interns participated in the Columbus school district's Peer Assistance and Review (PAR) program. Of these, 3,094 successfully completed the program, seventy-seven resigned before evaluation, ninety-one were not renewed, and fifty declined a contract offer.[7] These data are somewhat ambiguous, since some interns may have resigned to avoid a negative evaluation. We can assume, however, that the interns who declined contracts received favorable recommendations; but this raises an interesting point: How much of the cost of the program was wasted as a result of declinations by interns who received favorable evaluations?

Whatever the answer, 3,144 out of 3,312 Columbus interns (95 percent) were recommended for reemployment over the eleven-year period. As noted above (and as might be expected), about 92 percent of the interns in Toledo were also offered reemployment.

In some ways, the data on intervention in Columbus (shown in Table 2.2) are especially interesting. First, the total number of interventions was 178 over an eleven-year period, slightly over sixteen cases a year. In 1997–98, the district employed 4,600 teachers; using this number as the average for the preceding eleven years, there was one intervention annually for every 284 teachers. Interventions resulted in termination in only two cases during the eleven-year period. Although resignations and retirements may have been due to anticipated

Table 2.2.   Outcomes of PAR Intervention in Columbus,
1986–87 to 1996–97[8]

Outcomes over eleven years	Number	Percentage
Currently in Peer Assistance and Review (PAR) Program	13	7.3
Released in GOOD standing	78	43.8
Released in POOR standing/action pending	1	0.6
Released in POOR standing/resigned	15	8.4
Released in POOR standing/retired	3	1.7
Released in POOR standing/disability retirement	7	3.9
Released in POOR standing/nonrenewed	0	0.0
Released in POOR standing/terminated	2	1.1
Exited system while in the program/resigned	13	7.3
Exited system while in the program/retired	18	10.1
Exited system while in the program/disability retirement	27	15.2
Other	1	0.6
Total	**178**	

negative recommendations under peer review, intervention appears to play a very minor role in weeding out incompetent teachers. In fact, there is no evidence that peer review has resulted in more-stringent standards for dealing with tenured teachers whose performance has been called into question.

Clearly, most of the resources in the peer review plans are devoted to assisting and evaluating first-year teachers. The most important question would seem to be: What difference, if any, does peer review make in the proportion and quality of first-year teachers offered reemployment in Columbus? In the eleven years of peer review, 3,144 out of 3,312 new teachers were offered contracts at the conclusion of their first year; only 168, about 5 percent, either resigned before evaluation or were nonrenewed.

These data render it difficult to see how peer review could have made a significant difference in the quality of the Columbus teaching staff. Data on the procedure that was utilized in Columbus prior to peer review are not available. In view of the small percentage of teachers who resigned or were denied renewal under peer review, it is highly unlikely that peer review was more effective than conventional procedures in weeding out unqualified teachers. Instead, the union contends that peer review has helped the district improve and retain teachers who would otherwise go elsewhere or drop out of teaching.

In the overwhelming majority of cases, the renewal recommendations that result from peer review are probably the same as those that would have resulted under conventional procedures. This would probably have been true in Columbus even if every teacher receiving a negative recommendation under peer review would have received a favorable recommendation under conventional procedures, and vice versa. In fact, it is very probable that in the overwhelming majority of cases, both the peer review process and conventional evaluation would have been in agreement.

For all we know, peer review keeps incompetent teachers in the classroom longer than conventional procedures did or would. It is simply assumed that the recommendations under peer review are more reliable, but the assumption is not necessarily a fact. In view of the costs, which Chapter 6 shows to be considerable, peer review would have to display a significant margin of superiority to be justified. Peer review may be a superior personnel process overall, but no evidence unambiguously supports this conclusion.

3

Principals under Peer Review

In most schools, the principals evaluate teachers as part of their regular duties. Surprisingly, however, the implications of peer review for the role of principals are seldom discussed; for example, this issue was not mentioned in the debate over peer review at the 1997 NEA convention. Nevertheless, the topic deserves careful consideration.

Peer review raises several issues with respect to principals.

- Are consulting teachers more qualified than principals to evaluate new teachers?
- What is the impact of peer review on how principals allocate their time?
- To what extent do the recommendations of principals differ from those of consulting teachers, and how are such differences resolved?
- What is the impact of peer review on the principals' authority and leadership position?

To appreciate the importance of these issues, we must first review the status of supervisors under the state teacher bargaining laws. Under most of these laws, supervisors do not have bargaining rights. In most cases, principals are legally categorized as supervisors and are more directly affected by peer review than any other group of supervisors. Although the state bargaining laws differ, most have adopted the legal definition of "supervisor" that is found in the National Labor Relations Act (NLRA). For example, Ohio law provides that:

"[s]upervisor" means any individual who has authority, in the interest of the public employer, to hire, transfer, suspend, lay off, recall, promote, discharge, assign, reward, or discipline other public employees; to responsibly direct them; to adjust their grievances, or to effectively recommend such action, if the exercise of that authority is not of a merely routine or clerical nature but requires the use of independent judgment.[1]

Several aspects of this definition, as it has been interpreted and applied, merit our attention. One is that the authority to act on the employer's behalf is the critical factor. Whether that authority is actually exercised is not the decisive factor in determining supervisory status. Also, persons who spend most of their time in nonsupervisory duties are still supervisors if they have the requisite authority for a small portion of their work time. In order to be a supervisor, a person need have only one type of supervisory authority. To be specific, the fact that consulting teachers have the authority to effectively recommend dismissal is normally sufficient grounds to categorize them as supervisors. In fact, of all the kinds of authority that might be the basis for categorizing a person as a supervisor, the authority to make effective recommendations on dismissal is the most critical.

The phrase "to effectively recommend" does not mean that the recommendations must always be accepted. It is sufficient if they usually are. In the context of peer review, the consulting teachers would be supervisors even if school management had the legal authority to overrule their recommendations and sometimes did so.

The peer review dilemma should now be apparent. If the consulting teacher recommendations are effective, the consulting teachers should be categorized as supervisors; if they are supervisors, they are not covered by the bargaining laws and should not be in the same bargaining unit as regular teachers. Consequently, the consulting teachers would not be eligible for NEA or AFT membership as regular teachers. They could become NEA or AFT members only as members of a union of supervisory employees affiliated with the NEA or the AFT. To reiterate, the state bargaining laws often differ, but the majority have adopted or follow NLRA policy on supervisory issues.

When the NLRA was enacted in 1935, supervisors were covered by the act; that is, they had the right to form and join unions and engage in concerted activities. Employers, however, argued vehemently that they were entitled to the undivided loyalty of individuals acting on their behalf; moreover, there was a danger that employees would not be free to organize if supervisors were allowed to join their ranks. Thus, in 1947, Congress amended the NLRA as follows:

Nothing herein shall prohibit any individual employed as a supervisor from becoming or remaining a member of a labor organization, but no employer subject
to this Act shall be compelled to deem individuals defined herein as supervisors
as employees for the purpose of any law, either national or local, relating to collective bargaining.[2]

Consequently, supervisors are not prohibited from organizing or joining a
union, but employers need not bargain with supervisory unions or about the
terms and conditions of employment for supervisors. If these principles were
followed in public education, school boards would not be legally obligated to
bargain over the terms and conditions of employment for consulting teachers,
because the latter "effectively recommend" whether or not first-year teachers
should have their contracts renewed.

The legal implications of supervisory status are extremely important. Supervisors cannot require employers to recognize a union of supervisory employees, nor can supervisors be included in a bargaining unit with employees over
the objections of the employer. Furthermore, because supervisors are not covered employees, they can be fired for conduct that would not be cause for dismissal in the case of regular employees. The latter cannot be fired for trying to
organize a union; supervisors can be fired for doing so. This is only one example of the fact that supervisors cannot resort to charges of unfair labor practice
to uphold their statutory rights to organize and bargain collectively.

The union dilemma should now be apparent. On the one hand, peer review
is a process whereby consulting teachers and the union exercise responsibility
for terminating incompetent teachers. Insofar as this is the case, however, consulting teachers must be considered supervisors. In many states, the consulting
teachers would have to be dropped from the bargaining unit and would lose
their rights as employees under the state bargaining statutes. In some states, loss
of membership in the union would also be a logical corollary of supervisory status. The unions would lose the dues revenues from the consulting teachers, and
the latter would (or might) lose some of their influence in the union. The consulting teachers might welcome the double benefit of the consulting teacher
stipend and no payment of union dues, but the NEA and the AFT are not going
to push for reforms that lead to these outcomes. On the other hand, if consulting teachers and the union do not have the authority to effectively recommend
termination, the union claims for peer review cannot be sustained.

Peer review in Ohio resolved the supervisory dilemma through legislation.
In 1987, the state's bargaining statute was amended to shield the union and the
consulting teachers from the negative legal consequences of the supervisory
status of consulting teachers. The amendment to the Ohio public employee bargaining statute reads as follows:

The agreement may contain a provision that provides for a peer review plan under which public employees of a bargaining unit or representatives of an employee organization may, for other public employees of the same bargaining
unit or public employees whom the employee organization represents, participate in assisting, instructing, reviewing, evaluating, or appraising and make
recommendations or participate in decisions with respect to the retention, discharge, renewal, or non-renewal of, the public employees covered by a peer review plan.

The participation of a public employee or an employee organization representative in a peer review program permitted under this division shall not be construed as an unfair labor practice under this chapter or as a violation of any other
provision of law or rule adopted pursuant thereto.[3]

Section 4117.01 F(1) of this statute also provides that "[e]mployees of school
districts who are department chairmen or consulting teachers shall not be
deemed supervisors."

Under conventional arrangements, the principal is primarily responsible
for observing and evaluating new teachers, and for making recommendations
on their future employment status. Under the Toledo plan, however, the principal plays only a minor role in these matters insofar as first-year teachers are
concerned. The principal maintains the records on intern attendance and on
various noninstructional matters, but plays no role in observing and evaluating the interns' classroom performance. In the teachers' second year, however, the principals observe and evaluate the classroom performance of teachers; the consulting teachers are no longer in the picture except in unusual
cases. The principals' observations and evaluations utilize the same criteria
as were utilized by the consulting teachers in the interns' first year. Appendix E shows the limited scope of new teacher evaluations by principals in
Toledo. Interestingly enough, the union prefers evaluation by only one party
to avoid conflicting evaluations that would be conducive to litigation in termination situations.

It is interesting to compare the Toledo plan to the conventional union approach to probationary teachers. Usually, the unions try to reduce the amount
of time required to achieve tenure; their argument is that it does not or need not
require years to determine whether a teacher should be awarded tenure. Indeed,
some teacher union proposals would virtually eliminate probationary status and
provide first-year teachers with virtually the same protections as are accorded
to tenured teachers. Note, however, that eliminating the probationary period or
reducing it drastically would also eliminate or reduce the opportunities for paid
service as consulting teachers. It appears, therefore, that union positions on the
duration of the probationary period depend more on what is good for the union
and its senior teachers than on the amount of time required to evaluate new
teachers. If this is not the case, why do the unions try to reduce the probation-

ary period and the number of observations of new teachers to levels that are lower than those that would exist under peer review?

Setting costs aside, if peer review is more effective than conventional procedures in weeding out poor teachers, the reason may not be any superior competence of consulting teachers in evaluating teachers. The superiority, if it exists, may be due to two factors: first, under peer review, teachers lack the resources to challenge termination; and second, more time is devoted to observing and assisting teachers subject to peer review. Under conventional procedures, the union tries to limit the number of observations and evaluations as much as possible. When a teacher's competence becomes an issue, the union then argues that observations were too infrequent to justify termination, and it insists upon compliance with every procedural detail, no matter how irrelevant to the underlying competence issues.

Peer review changes the dynamics. Because consulting teachers benefit financially from peer review, an outcome made possible only by extensive observation and evaluation, the unions no longer keep the observations to a minimum; to the contrary, they now assert that frequent and longer observations are required for an entire school year.

Principals and Peer Review

We can take it for granted that the contractual provisions on peer review will vary; hence, so will their implications for principals. Moreover, the personality and responsibilities of principals will influence the way peer review affects them. Some principals may welcome peer review as a way to avoid confrontations with poor teachers; if the consulting teachers submit a favorable evaluation of poor teachers, the principals can hide behind the recommendations of the consulting teachers. In short, some principals may welcome peer review as a way to avoid confrontations with the union or teachers over negative evaluations and recommendations to fire the teachers.

Suppose there is a favorable evaluation by the consulting teacher but an unfavorable one by the principal. In this situation, it will be extremely difficult for the principal to sustain a negative recommendation. It is difficult enough when the principal has to overcome only the objections of the teacher being evaluated; when peer review enters the situation, the teachers being evaluated will rely on favorable recommendations by consulting teachers to rebut negative evaluations by principals.

To the extent that the principals' and consulting teachers' evaluations coincide, peer review merely adds another layer to the procedures for teacher evaluation. To the extent that the recommendations differ, it is essential to examine the reasons for and consequences of the differences. Regardless of the extent of the differences, however, peer review weakens the principals. It implies that principals are not carrying out their responsibilities effectively—hence the union is going to exercise these responsibilities with or without the principals. The union argument that principals are not effectively evaluating incompetent teachers may well be true, but the argument ignores the possibility that union obstruction is the reason. If it is, as is often the case, the solution is not necessarily for the union to assume supervisory duties. The solution may be for the union to cease and desist from the obstructive tactics that render it extremely difficult for principals to dismiss incompetent teachers.

Do Consulting Teachers Conduct Better Evaluations than Principals?

In leading peer review districts, the principals do not observe and evaluate first-year teachers in the classroom. The principals' role is limited to commenting about the way interns respond to rules and regulations, such as submission of reports in timely fashion.

Paradoxically, the literature on educational reform emphasizes the importance of principals. We are told repeatedly that principals must be instructional leaders and have ample authority to run their schools. Teacher evaluation is an important component of such authority, and principals (including assistant principals) conduct most of the teacher evaluations in public schools. In some of the larger districts and larger schools, specialists in various subjects and/or department chairmen evaluate teachers; but overall, principals conduct most of the evaluations in public schools. The union literature on peer review makes this point implicitly by contrasting peer review with evaluations by principals, not with evaluations by "supervisors."

Peer review, therefore, is a significant step away from the policies advocated by most education reformers. This does not mean that it is wrong, but it does suggest the need to scrutinize the implications of peer review for principals. The rationale for peer review assumes that the consulting teachers are more capable than principals of evaluating first-year teachers. This rationale is an article of faith that merits our scrutiny.

Preliminarily, we might note that many persons who cannot perform an activity, or cannot perform it very well, are nevertheless excellent teachers of it. The athletic world is replete with outstanding coaches who have not played for several decades. True, most previously played the sport they coach, but some average or even mediocre performers have become outstanding coaches. By the same token, not every outstanding player turns out to be an effective coach. Good coaching requires a knowledge of what it takes to play well. This is different from the ability to play well, although obviously these things are often closely related.

A critical point is that the coach's job, year in and year out, is to improve performance by players who can perform with training and to dismiss players who cannot achieve at acceptable levels, even with good coaching. Because the coach does this year in and year out, and because his own performance is based upon his success in carrying out these tasks, the coach has a huge personal stake in these tasks. This stake provides incentives to study all aspects of the player evaluation process—incentives that are broader and stronger than the incentives of good players who are asked occasionally to evaluate talent. In professional athletics, at least, not even the players assert that the judgments of active players (who have a huge stake in the success of the team) should supersede the personnel judgments of coaches. Similarly, it is not at all clear why the judgments of supervisors whose daily job is to evaluate teachers should be superseded by the judgments of teachers who go through a brief training period before evaluating teachers and who experience no risk to their own careers if they perform poorly at it. This is not to say that every principal is a more skilled evaluator than every consulting teacher in a peer review program, or even that most of them are. The point is that the assumption that regular classroom teachers are more skilled than principals in assisting and evaluating new teachers is dubious at best. The assumption appeals to teachers, especially since they can earn a substantial stipend based upon its validity, but it lacks either theoretical justification or supporting evidence.

Let us compare X, a principal, to Y, who becomes a consulting teacher after fifteen years in the classroom. Inasmuch as X has to evaluate teachers every year as part of his job, we can assume that X will have paid some attention to the professional literature on evaluation in his training and during his work as a principal. X's professional meetings and conferences will devote some attention to evaluation issues, and X will normally have much more evaluative experience than Y.

Until Y is selected as a consulting teacher, Y will have paid little or no attention to evaluation of other teachers. After all, in Toledo, the peer review plan assumes that Y can be trained to evaluate interns effectively with only two days of training—an assumption that leads one to wonder why principals cannot also master the subject before or during their principalship. Y observes nine teachers in each of his three years as a consulting teacher; X is likely to have evaluated many more in a single year, albeit for a shorter period of time than consulting teachers spend with interns.

The differences in incentives also suggest that principal X will usually be more effective than consulting teacher Y. Evaluation of interns and teachers in trouble is part of X's job; his entire career can be adversely affected if he does not perform well in this role. In contrast, Y is carrying out a temporary assignment that has no significant implications for Y's regular position. Y can walk away from the assignment at any time and revert to his regular position. X does not enjoy this privilege.

On some criteria, we can anticipate that the consulting teachers will normally be superior. For example, it appears likely that the consulting teachers will be more familiar than the principals with the subjects taught at the secondary level. Note, however, that large school districts often employ subject and grade-level supervisors who conduct evaluations along with the principals. Interestingly enough, in Toledo the principals, not the consulting teachers, have been the sole evaluators of the interns in their second probationary year.

No doubt, some principals are poor evaluators; that is a given in view of the fact that tens of thousands of principals evaluate teachers every year. It seems just as likely that if peer review becomes widespread, some consulting teachers would be incompetent in this role, but my point lies elsewhere. As matters stand, the unions have a vested interest in exaggerating the deficiencies of principals in evaluating teachers. By doing so, the union persuades teachers that support for the union is essential to protect teacher rights. If the unions stopped exaggerating the deficiencies of principals, the principals' credibility as evaluators might improve drastically. In short, the superior credibility of consulting teachers may be simply due to a union double standard in its attitude toward evaluators. The fact that the union-designated members of peer review governing boards virtually never disagree with the administrative members on renewal recommendations strongly supports this conclusion.

Under both peer review and managerial evaluation, a teacher can appeal his or her termination. Presumably, if a termination does not follow the appropriate criteria, whatever they are, the evaluations and any adverse actions based thereon will be overturned. But, if adherence to appropriate criteria is the ultimate test, why is it essential that teachers instead of administrators be the parties who apply the criteria at the operational level?

Toledo peer review pioneer Dal Lawrence states the reason as follows:

> During the intern year, the principal has only a very minimal role. He maintains a record of the intern's attendance and other noninstructional matters, but the development of the new teacher is in the hands of experienced colleagues. That's the way it should be. Principals don't teach school. And teachers, I should add, don't file reports with the state education department. You need good, competent people in both roles. We should stop this nonsense about a person who doesn't teach school being the instructional leader.[4]

Even if valid, the assumption that teachers are superior when it comes to evaluating other teachers does not necessarily justify peer review; other factors must be considered. But is the assumption valid? The criteria utilized to evaluate teachers in peer review districts are very similar to the criteria used in other districts. Any district can adopt and apply the criteria used to evaluate teachers in Toledo, Columbus, Rochester, or any other peer review district; the criteria are in the public domain and are available to everyone.

Furthermore, we must consider the implications of the tenure statutes for peer review. Inasmuch as most states have enacted tenure laws, the state courts are usually the terminal point of the appeal procedure when teachers challenge termination or nonrenewal of their contracts. Consequently, the statutory criteria for termination will be reflected in the peer review criteria. After all, a school district would be acting foolishly if it fired a teacher on the basis of criteria and procedures that are not consistent with the statutory tenure requirements. For this reason, the peer review process has to take the statutory requirements for dismissal into account. If the consulting teachers and review boards recommend termination on the basis of criteria that are not included in the tenure statute, their recommendations for termination will not be sustained if challenged in the courts.

In short, consulting teachers as well as school officials must operate within statutory limits that control the effectiveness of their recommendations to dismiss teachers. To the extent that this is true, it undermines the union claim that peer review will be more effective in terminating incompetent teachers. Whatever their views about teacher competence, the consulting teachers cannot apply them without regard to the statutory criteria for evaluating competence. The rhetoric of peer review suggests that the consulting teachers will be autonomous actors, applying professional standards to the evaluation process, but this will not be the reality in most situations. Generally speaking, the criteria under peer review are the same as the criteria in districts without peer review.

Consider a school district that averages ten cases a year in which dismissal is an issue. In the absence of peer review, principals and other school administrators will decide whether to recommend dismissal. In most cases, the answer will be obvious, one way or the other. Suppose that, on average, three cases a year are close calls. What will be the impact of peer review on this pattern? Will peer review result in a higher or lower number of close decisions? A higher or lower ratio of litigated decisions? A higher or lower average of successful challenges to recommendations to fire teachers? And if there are differences that support peer review, are the differences worth the additional costs, monetary and nonmonetary? These are some of the practical questions to be answered in considering peer review. At best, they are only rough guides to answering the question: To what extent, if any, does peer review result in improved instruction, and at what cost? In view of the NEA's enormous effort to promote peer review, the absence of any credible positive evidence on these issues is astonishing, but it seems highly probable that the outcomes under peer review do not differ materially from the outcomes under conventional evaluation procedures. Differences undoubtedly will exist, but they are most likely to arise in marginal cases on which reasonable persons can disagree. If there are any significant positive differences, they are probably due to the fact that school administrators are more likely to recommend dismissal if they know that the teacher union supports or at least will not contest a termination. In other words, peer review does not necessarily reflect any significant differences in administrator/teacher judgments about competence. Instead, it may function as a signal to the administration that it can fire a teacher without encountering union opposition. At best, this is a weak argument for peer review, since it is practicable to reach the same result without the heavy costs of peer review.

The proportion of poor teachers is a matter of dispute, but there is widespread agreement that it is too high. The most common reason is that school administrators are unwilling to face the intense union opposition that follows recommendations to fire teachers. This may be deplorable, but it is a fact of life in schools. Prior to their support for peer review, the unions asserted that their role is merely to provide due process for teachers facing dismissal. According to this rationale, union opposition to teacher terminations was said to be inherent in the union role. In contrast, under peer review, the union's obligation is not to ensure due process by representing teachers facing termination charges, but to ensure due process by union participation in the proceedings leading up to termination.

If the criteria under peer review are the same as under conventional procedures, wherein lies the superior effectiveness of the consulting teachers? It would have to lie in their superior skill in applying the criteria, but there is no research that supports this conclusion. As one NEA member opposed to peer review bluntly commented:

> A teacher-driven dismissal system might not be any better than the present dismissal system. Principals are trained and certified to evaluate. There's no evidence to show that teachers with little evaluation training will do a better job. If they can, then we've wasted tons of money on principal-training programs.
>
> It makes no sense to train teachers as evaluators if they're simply going to do the same thing that principals are already doing. Reformers who argue that the system isn't working should focus on fixing the poor performance of the principals rather than creating new teams of teachers to perpetuate the same mistakes.
>
> Finally, does anyone believe that the teachers who are selected to become judges of their colleagues are going to be any less influenced than principals by bias, pettiness, and political pressures?[5]

According to Lawrence, the Toledo principals were initially opposed to peer review, but eventually became supporters of it. This claim is hardly persuasive, especially in view of the fact that the Toledo school district sought vigorously to strengthen the role of principals in teacher evaluation in the 1997 negotiations between the district and the TFT. The unions assert that whatever may be the theory, principals are not generally held accountable for the low quality of their evaluations. Undoubtedly, this is often true. It does not follow, however, that peer review is the appropriate remedy.

In conventional evaluation by principals, the absence of accountability is not due to a deficiency in the administrative structure. When a principal evaluates teachers poorly, but without any adverse consequences to the principal, the solution may be a change in personnel, or a change in union programs that make it difficult to impose disciplinary action. The lack of accountability under peer review, however, is built into the structure.

Theoretically, consulting teachers are accountable to the Board of Review (by whatever title), but the board has no way of monitoring the work of consulting teachers. It can transfer a consulting teacher back to the classroom, but this means only that the worst thing that can happen to a consulting teacher is to get his or her job back at the regular salary.

This brings us to what is perhaps the strongest objection to peer review. The teacher unions support it on the grounds that they have a responsibility to help incompetent teachers or guide them into another field. The unions seek to implement their newly discovered responsibility by union co-determination of what were formerly regarded as management decisions. Such co-determination is likely to erode, not raise, the standards for teaching positions. The reason is that teachers are not likely to impose high standards that could boomerang against themselves. We can see this in the fact that tenured teachers are seldom evaluated in the leading peer review districts. As a matter of fact, more than 1,100 tenured teachers in Toledo are never evaluated; in 1997, some had not been evaluated since 1970.[6] The same lowering of standards under group responsibility is especially evident in higher education. When faculties draw up the rules governing office hours or outside employment or conflicts of interest with faculty obligations, the rules are much less stringent than when they are made by the administration. Consulting teachers may adopt high standards for interns, knowing that the standards do not apply to themselves or to regular faculty, but neither theory nor practice indicates that we can raise the quality of most teachers this way. The underlying issue is whether the teacher unions should exercise managerial functions, or whether they can drop their excessive obstruction of managerial performance of managerial functions without compromising their role as protector of employee interests.

4

Professionalism and Accountability

The proponents of peer review assert that it is a step toward professional status for teachers. The idea is that "professions" are occupational groups that accept collective responsibility for maintaining high standards of competence. Supposedly, medical societies and bar associations illustrate this point.

As we have seen, the teacher unions have been widely criticized for their obstructionist role in efforts to fire incompetent teachers. The union response has been that the unions are not trying to defend incompetent teachers. Instead, they are trying to ensure that teachers charged with incompetence receive due process if they wish to challenge the charges. The union view is that if incompetent teachers cannot be fired because they have not received due process, the fault for their continued employment lies with the school administration, not the union. Peer review, however, is supposed to reflect a "professional" approach, whereby teachers exercise responsibility for maintaining high standards for teachers. Unfortunately, peer review is irrelevant to professionalism in theory and in practice.

Peer review as a process for screening new teachers illustrates this point. New teachers subject to peer review already have a teaching certificate. The only employment issue to be resolved under peer review is whether the new teacher will be employed by school district X. Even if district X does not employ the teacher, the latter is a member of the profession and is free to accept employment as a teacher anywhere in the state. In states that have reciprocity with other states, the new teacher can accept employment in other states as well.

This is very different from failure to pass a state bar examination; in the latter case, the individual cannot serve as an attorney anywhere in the state. In short, peer review affects only employment decisions by individual school districts; negative reviews and termination of employment in a peer review district do not prevent new teachers from teaching elsewhere in the state. The same point applies to veteran teachers whose employment has been terminated under peer review.

Ohio has enacted legislation that envisages the statewide adoption of peer review for first-year teachers in less than ten years. Consider the following problems with such legislation.

1. Under statewide peer review, it would be practically impossible to implement a consistent set of standards for a teaching certificate. For the sake of discussion, assume that all districts in Ohio use the same evaluation form for evaluating first-year teachers. That is, assume that the formally stated criteria are the same in every school district—an assumption which is not likely to prevail in practice in the overwhelming majority of states. Even on the basis of this assumption, we can anticipate wide variation in how the criteria are applied to intern teachers. First, there is no mechanism to assure a consistent approach from one district to another. The model peer review districts have a program to facilitate consistency among their consulting teachers, but there is no persuasive evidence that it is effective in this regard. In any case, a statewide program to achieve consistency between school districts, instead of within them, raises a host of problems. Every year, thousands of teachers scattered over the state would have to undergo a training program to achieve a defensible level of consistency in applying the criteria. Who will sponsor and who will pay how much for such a program, with what likelihood of achieving the objective?

2. In the occupations recognized as professions, a state examination is administered and scored by a single state agency; the possibility of inconsistent applications of the same criteria is minimal or does not arise. Under peer review, however, the standards will inevitably be affected by supply-and-demand factors from district to district. A district that is experiencing severe shortages in recruiting teachers to teach a particular subject is bound to apply less rigorous criteria than a district that is not subject to such shortages. School districts experiencing difficulty in recruiting teachers will inevitably lower their standards to attract teachers. This happens now even in the absence of peer review.

3. Statewide peer review does not address certification of teachers who want to move to Ohio. An out-of-state teacher with a good record is not likely to move to a state in which continued employment as a teacher de-

pends on a favorable recommendation from a peer review school district. On the other hand, if there is reciprocity in certification, many teachers will seek employment first outside the peer review state. This would not be in the state's interest. In view of the substantial interstate migration of teachers, this issue will have to be faced, but it is difficult to see how it can be resolved without major negative consequences. If the solution is to accept "successful" teaching experience in other states as the basis for issuing a certificate, the variability will be tremendous. After all, it is common practice to give poor or marginal teachers rather favorable evaluations so they can get teaching jobs elsewhere. Agreements to this effect ("Resign and we won't destroy your chances of getting a position elsewhere") are not formalized, but few if any school administrators will deny that this scenario happens frequently. If evaluations of interns are converted to tests of eligibility to teach anywhere in the state, tens of thousands of teachers will be making critical career decisions affecting hundreds of thousands of teachers annually, without any personal accountability for the quality of the decisions. This is a drastically different type of control from situations in which a state professional organization arranges for a single test applied uniformly throughout the state.

4. Statewide peer review legislation would not apply to private schools. The latter can usually employ teachers who are not certified—a huge difference from the recognized professions. Private hospitals cannot employ noncertified physicians; unlicensed personnel cannot legally practice dentistry or law. The point is not that private schools should be required to employ only certified teachers; on the contrary, my position is that certification is a highly unreliable guide to teaching competence. Be that as it may, peer review cannot be equated with collective professional responsibility for standards.

As of early 1998, no peer review plan had any authority to exclude a teacher from teaching elsewhere. At most, peer review is a procedure to decide whether teachers will be employed by a particular school district. It may or may not be justified on this basis, but it cannot be justified as a step toward "professionalism." If it can be justified at all, it can be justified only as an employment procedure, and whether it can be justified as an employment procedure is highly debatable. Does the total cost of peer review increase the accuracy of employment decisions sufficiently to justify the costs? This question leads to a corollary one: Are there alternative ways to improve employment decisions at a lower cost? Interestingly enough, despite the fact that the Toledo program has been in effect since 1981 and the Columbus program since 1986, there is no comprehensive analysis of the costs of either program. One must wonder about the advisability of adopting basic changes in personnel policy without facing cost issues.

Accountability under Peer Review

The supporters of peer review contend that it will make teachers "accountable." Because they never define the term, it is impossible to evaluate the alleged benefit; however, the following definition probably incorporates the idea that most citizens have in mind when they use the term. "Accountability" means that an actor is subject to negative consequences for failure to act competently or ethically. The negative consequences may be inflicted by a market system, by a political system, or by individuals empowered to inflict the negative consequences upon the actor.

The idea is simple enough. We say that elected officials are "accountable" because they can be voted out of office. In the economic arena, accountability is based upon performance in competitive markets. Inferior or more expensive products lose out to better or less expensive ones; accountability is consumer driven. And in employment relations, accountability means that individual employees are subject to adverse consequences for poor performance by parties authorized to inflict such consequences. If you do not show up for work on time, or your work is of poor quality, you can be disciplined by someone with the authority to hold you "accountable."

As I use the term, "accountability" means responsibility for actions. If a group takes responsibility, the group must be subject to negative consequences, or there is no accountability. Again, responsibility for actions means that the actor(s) are personally subject to adverse consequences. "Adverse consequences" in the employment context does not mean consequences to society or to a group. It means that the actors can suffer loss of pay or some concrete benefit associated with their jobs. Individuals are not accountable merely because they are members of a group that experiences adverse consequences as a result of their actions. Generals are not accountable merely because their nation suffers from their poor leadership; likewise, teachers are not accountable simply because their fellow teachers or their school districts or communities are worse off as a result of the teachers' actions. As a matter of fact, individuals often benefit from actions that have adverse consequences for the groups to which they belong.

Consider the system of accountability that peer review is intended to supplant or replace. In most situations, principals are required to evaluate first-year teachers. Such evaluation is part of the principal's job. If principals do not evaluate teachers fairly and competently, we can say that the principals are not doing their job adequately. Of course, this is a reason for school management to remove the principals from office. The principals are accountable to higher levels of school management for competent performance.

Where is the accountability under peer review? The consulting teachers are provided released time with pay to observe, assist, and evaluate beginning teachers. To whom are these consulting teachers accountable, and for what? Based upon the practice of peer review to date, the answer is that they are not accountable to anyone for their performance in this role. First of all, the districts that have adopted peer review do not include performance as a consulting teacher on the latter's evaluation form. According to the rhetoric, the consulting teachers are outstanding teachers who volunteer for the assignment and are motivated by the desire to raise standards. Surely, however, no one will contend that all consulting teachers always perform in this role at acceptable levels. Because service as a consulting teacher is often a much easier assignment than teaching classes, some teachers will see such service as an escape hatch. Some will be overburdened with their professional or family duties. Some will act or be accused of acting in a racially or sexually discriminatory way. Even the most prominent supporters of peer review concede that its financial rewards motivate many teachers to serve as consulting teachers. I am not asserting that most consulting teachers are incompetent; I am asserting only that we cannot expect every consulting teacher to perform competently, any more than we can expect every principal to do so. If this is the case, and how can it be otherwise, where is the accountability for poor performance as a consulting teacher?

To whom are the consulting teachers accountable? Certainly, they are not accountable to the union; the union has no authority by itself to deprive a consulting teacher of any benefit; the union's role is to protect consulting teachers, not discipline them for unsatisfactory performance. The debate over peer review at the 1997 NEA convention was largely about protecting consulting teachers from lawsuits; the rights of the teachers subject to peer review were a secondary concern.

It is difficult to see how a school district could hold consulting teachers accountable for their performance in this capacity. The fact that regular teacher evaluation forms do not cover performance as a consulting teacher is indicative of the lack of accountability in peer review. There does not appear to be a single district that has developed standards for performance for consulting teachers. Furthermore, it is not clear how accountability would be implemented. Who would evaluate the performance of the consulting teachers, and on what basis? With principals, there is a track record; most evaluate ten to twenty-five teachers annually year after year; hence, it is possible to compare their evaluations of teachers with teacher performance over a period of years. It is practically impossible to do this for consulting teachers because of the lack of an adequate data base for each consulting teacher.

Suppose a consulting teacher submits favorable recommendations for interns who turn out to be poor teachers. By the time this is evident, the consulting teacher will often have returned to his or her regular position. Absent some especially egregious conduct by consulting teachers, it is virtually impossible to evaluate their performance. The teachers being assisted or evaluated may leave district employment for reasons that have nothing to do with their teaching performance. Their teaching may become inadequate for several reasons that would not justify adverse action against their consulting teachers. With principals, however, there is a data base on which we can reasonably evaluate their performance in assisting/evaluating new teachers; this is not so in the case of consulting teachers who assist and/or evaluate a much smaller number of teachers for three years or less.

At the 1997 NEA convention, it was assumed that some consulting teachers would be challenged, even sued, on account of their conduct in this role. Suppose a new teacher subject to peer review files a grievance, alleging that the peer review process was flawed in a way that resulted in major career harm to the grievant. Whom does the union support—the grievant, or the consulting teachers? The consulting teachers will be the more senior teachers, designated as consultants by the union or with union approval. The union will want to avoid placing itself in a position in which it must try to sustain a grievance against senior teachers, especially since such teachers usually play a dominant role in the union. In practice, the grievance might be against the school district for taking an adverse action, such as denial of reemployment, but the basis for the grievance would be the school district's reliance on consulting teachers who performed their task unsatisfactorily. For this reason, the union could not concede that the grievance has merit without impugning the performance of the consulting teachers. Realistically, this is not going to happen very often. In Rochester, New York, the Rochester Teachers Association (RTA) provided legal help to the consulting teachers, while its state affiliate provided legal help to a grievant in the same case. The Peer Assistance and Review (PAR) Program in Columbus theoretically formalizes such an arrangement; if a teacher challenges an adverse recommendation by the PAR governing board, the Ohio Education Association represents the teacher and is reimbursed by the Columbus Education Association for doing so. It is difficult to see how a teacher could have any confidence in representation by the state affiliate of a local union that has decided, in effect, that the teacher's case is not meritorious. From the teacher's standpoint, a much better solution would be for the union to pay for legal counsel chosen by the teacher.

Peer Review as Assistance

In the labor relations environment, there is a huge difference between:

(1) "Consulting teachers X, Y, and Z helped teachers A, B, and C to improve," and
(2) "Consulting teachers X, Y, and Z recommend that teachers A, B, and C not be rehired for the following reasons," and then having the reasons spelled out.

The first alternative avoids most of the problems associated with peer review as an evaluation process; however, if peer review is limited to assistance at district expense, it should be recognized for what it is: a procedure whereby teachers are relieved of their classroom duties to help other teachers, but have no responsibility for recommendations regarding the employment status of the teacher receiving assistance.

The question is whether district funds spent this way will be very useful. The answer will depend on several factors, especially the amount of time the consulting teachers spend with the teachers receiving assistance. A few hours may be worthwhile; a few months may not be. Also, we should not overlook the fact that the consulting teacher will be away from his or her regular classes; the costs of substitutes and the disruptions to the consulting teacher's regular classes must be considered. These negatives are not an issue when principals are responsible for assistance and evaluation. The principal who assists teachers to improve has a career stake in the outcome; principals who do not help poor teachers to improve are on shaky career grounds. In contrast, the consulting teachers are evaluated, if they are evaluated at all, on the basis of their regular teaching, not on the quality of their assistance to new teachers.

It is often alleged that teachers are accountable because their school or the teaching profession will suffer if teachers do not help to weed out poor teachers. Fortunately, this concept of accountability does not permeate our military services. This crucial point cannot be overemphasized: Teachers are not accountable because the nation or their school district or their school or their students will suffer negative consequences as a result of poor teacher performance. There is accountability only if the teachers who perform poorly suffer adverse consequences personally as a result of their own actions. A good teacher in a poor school should not be subjected to negative consequences; a poor teacher in a good school should not get immunity because of the good work of other teachers.

To summarize, the notion that peer review shows that teachers are maturing as a profession is based upon misconceptions about the professions and about accountability. For that matter, such "maturity," if it materialized, would be a step backward in public policy. Doctors, lawyers, and other so-called "professional" groups have utilized control over entry more to enrich themselves than to protect the public. There is no reason to assume that teacher control over entry into teaching would lead to a different outcome, and much reason to conclude that it would lead to the same outcome.

In some respects, the basic issue in peer review appears to be whether it is possible to reconcile the concept of a union, legally and practically responsible for promoting the interests of its members, with the concept of a professional organization. This depends on how we define "professional organization." If it is defined as an organization designed to protect the public, as NEA publications imply, we must bear in mind that "professional" organizations eventually become as self-serving as unions. At some points, the interests of occupational organizations conflict with the public interest; the proposition that what is good for teachers is good for the country is as absurd in education as it is in every other field.

This does not mean that teacher and union interests always conflict with the public interest. Whether such conflict exists can be determined only by analyzing the facts of each case; it is fair to say, however, that a potential conflict is present in every situation. Granted, there is probably no organization that does not favor its own interests over the public interest on some issues. Even religious orders that have adopted vows of poverty have interests in organizational survival that may conflict with the public interest. Furthermore, no organization is completely free to resolve conflicts of interest in favor of its own welfare and/or the welfare of its members. Regardless of why the NEA and the AFT are promoting peer review, does peer review resolve any conflict between the union interest and the public interest in favor of the latter?

It is difficult to see how it does so. Peer review may enhance the teacher union image, but it does so only by obscuring the basic issues that it raises. In view of the enormous union resources devoted to media and public opinion, the NEA and the AFT may experience some success in promoting peer review, but media gullibility is the major reason for peer review's visibility as a step toward "professional" status.

5

Due Process and the Duty of Fair Representation under Peer Review

In the past, the NEA and the AFT have vigorously rejected criticisms of their role in defending teachers charged with incompetence. The union position has always been that its role is not to defend incompetence but to ensure that teachers charged with it receive due process in defending themselves. The context may be a grievance hearing before an arbitrator or a court case before a jury, but the union's role is supposed to be ensuring due process in both.

"Due process" is essentially the idea of fairness. When dismissal is the issue, due process includes notice of the charges, a right to a hearing before an impartial arbitrator or jury, and the opportunity to confront adverse witnesses and introduce witnesses and evidence to support the defense. Each of these elements is or can be subject to controversy; for example, how many observations of what duration constitute an adequate basis for evaluating classroom performance?

Because charges of incompetence have such important adverse consequences if sustained, courts and arbitrators usually require high standards of compliance with procedural requirements. If a contract calls for observations of thirty uninterrupted minutes, an observation of twenty-nine minutes will be deemed insufficient. Insistence upon such procedural requirements often is at the heart of criticisms of the teacher unions; in the latter's view, however, they are simply insisting upon full compliance with due process. Failure to adhere to contractual or statutory procedures has been deemed to be management's responsibility, not the unions'. Furthermore, the unions have contended that any failure on their part to utilize every argument possible would subject them to penalties for violating their duty of fair representation.

Peer review constitutes a break from this traditional union position. The unions still acknowledge their responsibility to ensure "due process," but they no longer argue that dismissing incompetent teachers is solely management's responsibility. The union is said to have an affirmative obligation to help teachers become competent or guide them out of the profession. The obvious problem that arises is how to reconcile the representative role with the newly adopted professional role. It is as if your lawyer suddenly announced that because our judicial system was breaking down, his responsibility was not only to represent you to the best of his ability, but also to ensure that you did not take advantage of various legal loopholes to avoid the outcome you may deserve.

Despite widespread opinion to the contrary, the unions are not required to process every grievance; they are not even required to process every meritorious grievance. For instance, suppose a teacher entitled to a thirty-minute duty-free lunch was asked to keep an eye on a disruptive student in the cafeteria. Suppose also that most teachers are actually enjoying a forty-five-minute duty-free lunch that is coming under criticism by school administrators. Processing the grievance might jeopardize a larger benefit for most teachers; hence, the union would not necessarily violate the duty of fair representation by not pursuing the grievance to arbitration. The union would, however, violate the duty of fair representation if it refused to process a grievance for a nonmember while pursuing the same grievance on behalf of union members.

Of course, whenever discretion is present, there is a possibility that it will be abused. Nonetheless, it is unlikely that teacher unions would be violating their duty of fair representation by declining to process a grievance challenging a peer review recommendation to fire the grievant. As long as the peer review program provided due process, a union could probably avoid or prevail in litigation which alleged that the union's refusal to represent teachers facing dismissal violates its duty of fair representation. As we have seen, however, the Ohio bargaining law was amended to allow unions and teachers to participate in peer review plans without being subject to unfair labor practice charges as a result of such participation.[1]

Despite the enactment of the amendment, the Toledo Federation of Teachers (TFT) asserted the following to the fact finder when its negotiations with the school district reached an impasse in 1997:

> In this traditional evaluation approach, the union is required by DFR [duty of fair representation] decisions to represent nearly all members evaluated as poor

performers or those targeted for non-renewal or termination if they come to the
union for help. The vigorous conflict these cases engender is one of the fuels
that drives animosity between labor and management. It is a teacher-adminis-
trator relationship absent of support from the nation's leading education reform
experts.[2]

In short, the TFT relied upon a legal argument that it knew was not applicable to the Toledo situation; the TFT was not required by the duty of fair
representation to represent teachers "evaluated as poor performers or . . . targeted for non-renewal or termination if they come to the union for help."
Even in the absence of the statutory amendment, however, the union is not
required to represent teachers without regard to the strength of the case for
terminating them. The teacher's right to due process does not require the
union to press every line of defense to the limit, no matter how weak the argument for doing so.

Due Process under Peer Review

The supporters of peer review contend that the union can meet its obligation to provide due process under peer review. The consulting teachers first
try to help the interns to perform adequately. If the interns fail to improve, the
consulting teachers inform the interns of the negative evaluations and provide
them opportunities to respond. If the school administration accepts the recommendation not to renew, the interns have the right to be given notice, a
hearing, and an opportunity to rebut the negative evidence presented to the
school officials who must approve the recommendation not to renew. Allegedly, these safeguards meet the union's obligation to provide due process
under peer review.

The fact is, however, that the interns subject to peer review have less protection than they have in its absence. To see why, let us assume that the Board
of Review approves a consulting teacher's recommendation that X's contract
not be renewed. X, however, believes that the recommendation is not justified.
To whom does X turn for help to argue his case? Toledo and Columbus illustrate two different answers to this question. In Toledo, an intern can appeal a
negative recommendation to the union executive board, but the board will not
support the intern if the proper procedures were followed throughout the
process.

For the sake of discussion, assume that the union can legally meet its obligation to provide due process in a peer review program. Note, however, the

practical difference in the two situations. In the conventional situation, the union represents the teacher if the school administrator recommends dismissal. Consequently, the teacher has experienced, skilled representation in the dismissal proceedings. Not so under peer review. The union does not come to the aid of the teacher; the latter is left to fight the adverse evaluation from personal resources.

Significantly, the NEA successfully argued before the U.S. Supreme Court that the NEA should be viewed as a reserve force, ready to be called upon as needed. The issue arose in litigation over agency shop fees; the question was whether nonmembers could be required to pay service fees to the NEA and the state associations as well as to a local association. It is difficult to see how the NEA or the AFT can justify taking dues and agency fees and then drastically changing the rules governing who is entitled to union services. To many in and out of the NEA and the AFT, it seems unfair to deny teachers who have paid their dues for many years the benefits of union representation just when it is most needed. Perhaps it would be more equitable to deny union representation to teachers who were informed from the outset that the union would not represent them in challenges to intervention dismissals. It will be interesting to see how these issues play out as the NEA aggressively promotes peer review.

One's reaction may be: So what? If the union supports instead of opposes dismissal of incompetent teachers, should we not applaud the change? It seems inconsistent to accuse the unions of excessive protection of incompetent teachers and then criticize them for making it easier to dismiss such teachers. The answer is, however, that peer review is a poor way to eliminate excessive union protection of incompetent teachers. To cite just one possibility, the unions might accept binding arbitration of statutory tenure disputes, so that school districts would not face protracted litigation in efforts to fire incompetent teachers.

Under peer review the union acts as a prosecutor, not as the representative of the defendant. Requiring the intern to pay only half the regular dues does not fully address the problem because the unavailability of union representation in dismissals is only part of the problem. The Toledo Federation of Teachers has reduced union dues by half for interns because it will not represent teachers who challenge a negative recommendation by the Board of Review. The implication is that the union can split up its core functions and charge members according to the functions provided to different groups of members. If the union can decline to represent members in a dismissal case by waiving a specified portion of regular dues, can it decline to represent some members with respect to other issues, such as salaries, by reducing union dues to compensate for the services not provided? If not, why not?

It must be emphasized that the peer review situation differs from the common practice of union-sponsored benefits. It is very common for unions to offer benefits open only to union members. For example, the NEA and the AFT offer dozens of supplemental services that their members can purchase from personal funds. However, the benefits open only to union members who pay for them are not offered in lieu of core union functions, such as protection against dismissal. With respect to these supplemental benefits, the union is merely serving as a vendor, because it is in a good position to take advantage of its mass purchasing power. The member buys a service or product from the union, which competes against other vendors of the same or similar products and services.

It would be quite a stretch, however, to equate the peer review arrangement with union-sponsored supplemental benefits. True, the intern can go into the market to find an attorney to represent the intern in challenging the nonrenewal. However, consider the practical realities. The 1997–98 dues in the TFT were approximately $520.[3] The intern pays only $260. It is very unlikely that the intern could find competent representation for $260. Clearly, this is out of the question if the expenses of trials, depositions, discovery, and legal appeals are taken into account.

Furthermore, if the union is allowed to pick and choose what core services it will provide, the individuals who are excluded from such services are at a severe disadvantage in resolving the appropriate amount to be deducted from regular dues. In the first fifteen years of the Toledo plan, only two interns challenged a Board of Review recommendation not to renew. On the other hand, the TFT collected half of the regular dues from the interns.

At first glance, it appears that the interns are getting a very good deal: they pay only $260 for services worth $520. Closer scrutiny provides a dramatically different perspective. The regular members pay $520 for the same services that the interns get (minus one service that costs the union only a minuscule amount) for $260. After all, the union would very rarely have to devote any of its resources to termination cases involving interns. Put in another way, the regular teachers pay $520, interns $260, with the only difference being that the interns are not entitled to a service that costs the union $5 to $10 at most. If the TFT arrangement for interns reflects the actual value of union services, members are being heavily overcharged for them.

The dubious allocation of dues in Toledo underscores a critical point about the relationships between peer review and the duty of fair representation. These relationships create internal as well as legal problems for the unions. In some situations, any resolution of the problem may have an adverse effect on membership. This is less likely to happen where the teacher unions have negotiated an agency fee clause, as they have in Toledo, Columbus, and Rochester. In districts where members can resign from the union without having to pay the agency fee, it is likely that disagreements over fair representation and dues would probably have a negative impact on membership.

The Duty of Fair Representation in Columbus

We have yet to consider how the duty of fair representation is resolved in Columbus. In that district, the teacher who wishes to contest a recommendation not to rehire is entitled to union support, but it is provided by the Ohio Education Association (OEA) through an arrangement with the CEA. In other words, the CEA contracts out the actual defense of the teacher to its state affiliate.

Understandably, teachers will view this arrangement skeptically; there is a conflict of interest in having the OEA represent a teacher who is, in effect, challenging a recommendation supported by the OEA's largest affiliate. An alternative resolution would be to give the teacher a lump sum for legal representation and allow the teacher to select his or her own legal counsel, but this solution has problems of its own. Obviously, one is the amount; the higher the amount, the less attractive this solution will be to the unions. A solution whereby the union adequately funds litigants against the union is not likely to survive if activated in more than a minuscule number of cases.

Significantly, if a local union initiates a peer review plan, its insurance costs increase. Prior to the 1997 NEA convention, NEA insurance policies could not provide protection for consulting teachers in that capacity; after the adoption of Resolution New D-6 at the 1997 convention, it was possible for state affiliates to buy peer review insurance to protect the consulting teachers. Consequently, by 1997, ten state affiliates had signed up for the supplemental insurance. In view of the fact that the cost of the insurance averaged only fifteen cents per member, the fact that only ten states had purchased it suggests a slow rate of acceptance of peer review within the NEA itself. At the 1997 NEA convention, Robert H. Chanin, the NEA's General Counsel, was asked to explain the legal issues relating to the union's duty of fair representation. In his explanation, Chanin emphasized that the duty does not require the union to represent every teacher charged with incompetence. The union is required only to ensure that each teacher receives due process. Significantly, the NEA decided not to make Chanin's convention comments about peer review available to delegates in written form. This deviation from the practice of making convention addresses available to delegates and members in written form reflects the legal uncertainties surrounding the matter; Chanin did point out, however, that the small number of legal cases on the duty of fair representation may be the reason that so many legal issues are still unresolved. It should be noted, however, that issues relating to the duty of fair representation would not arise in states that had not enacted a bargaining law.

For that matter, peer review itself is not likely to arise in states that have not authorized teacher bargaining. The reason is that the unions need to structure peer review in ways that protect the unions from liability for deficiencies in the peer review process. Bargaining laws provide the opportunities to negotiate such ways of protecting the unions. In other words, despite the rhetoric to the effect that peer review is a step toward professional accountability, it is actually a step in the opposite direction.

6

The Costs of Peer Review

As with any personnel process, there are costs to peer review. Our choice is not between a process that involves costs and one that is cost-free. It is how best to maximize sound personnel decisions at a reasonable cost. It is almost always possible to improve the quality of personnel decisions if costs are irrelevant, but that is rarely the case. For example, in deciding whom to employ, a school district might check out ten references instead of three, but the improvement in hiring decisions might not be worth the additional costs.

A 1984 analysis by the Rand Corporation estimated the cost of peer review in Toledo to be $2,000 per intern in 1983–84. Aside from the outdated price level, the estimate was egregiously deficient.[1] For example, it included the costs of the substitutes for the consulting teachers instead of the costs of the consulting teachers themselves; because this error often characterizes the few references to the costs of peer review, it is essential to clarify the issue.

The proponents of peer review interpret its costs as the additional expenditures required to implement peer review. This way of interpreting costs overlooks the change in the purpose of expenditures. When a new teacher is employed at $25,000 to substitute for a $50,000 consulting teacher, the cost of peer review is the $50,000 paid to the consulting teacher, not the $25,000 paid to the consulting teacher's substitute. Furthermore, the Rand estimate did not include the costs of administrator time or the travel reimbursements to the consulting teachers, or the increases in district contributions for retirement, to cite just a few more obvious omissions.

If we do not know the costs, it is hardly possible to assert with any confidence that the benefits of peer review are worth the costs. After all, even if peer review has beneficial outcomes, the issue is whether the additional costs could bring about even more benefits if spent in some other way. Unfortunately, the neglect of costs is a major oversight in the favorable treatment of peer review, but the importance of the issue should be manifest.[2]

A preliminary list of the costs of peer review includes the following:

- Salaries and fringe benefits for consulting teachers. "Fringe benefits" are normally construed to include payments for pensions, insurance (including health insurance), leaves of all kinds, holiday and vacation pay, and a host of additional items such as severance pay, or tuition reimbursement.
- Salaries and fringe benefits for administrators who serve on the Board of Review or a similar body (by whatever title it is known). Of course, the costs of administrative time must reflect only the time they devote to peer review.
- The costs for the union-designated members on the Board of Review who are employed by the district. Insofar as these members are employed by the school district, the costs of their time, not the costs of their substitutes, should be charged to peer review.
- Mileage for consulting teachers who travel to different schools.
- Legal costs associated with peer review issues, such as determining peer review's consistency with the duty of fair representation or the implications of due process for a peer review plan.
- Overhead costs, such as the costs of clerical/secretarial help, copying, telephone calls, and postage.
- Additional liability insurance for consulting teachers.

Some brief comments about a few of these costs may provide some idea of their magnitudes. Of course, any savings or improvements in outcomes must be factored into the analysis, but let us first try to assess the costs.

Consulting Teacher Salaries and Fringe Benefits

The salaries and fringe benefits for consulting teachers are the major costs of peer review. Understandably, consulting teachers tend to be senior teachers who are among the highest paid in the district. In Toledo, the 1997–98 salary schedule for teachers with an M.A. degree ranged from $25,777 to $47,194. The stipend for consulting teachers is renegotiated with each new contract between the Toledo Federation of Teachers (TFT) and the board of education; in 1997–98, the stipend was $5,000 above the teacher's regular salary.

The regular teacher salary schedule in Columbus is slightly higher than the Toledo schedule, but the Columbus stipend for consulting teachers is set at 20 percent of the base salary for a beginning teacher with a B.A. degree. For

1997–98, the stipend in Columbus is 20 percent of $29,403, or $5,881 above the consulting teacher's regular salary. The single most important difference between the Columbus and Toledo plans is not the compensation of consulting teachers but their workload. Consulting teachers in Columbus work with eighteen interns, or fifteen interns plus one teacher in intervention. In Toledo, there is no rigid formula, but the consulting teachers normally work with nine interns. This is a huge difference that is not addressed in the literature on the two programs. Because of an unusually large number of new teachers in 1997–98, each Toledo consulting teacher supervised thirteen interns. This raises a question: If each consulting teacher can supervise thirteen interns adequately, why does the program normally utilize a nine-to-one ratio?

Retirement costs consist of the contributions by school districts and states to teacher retirement. The contributions in Ohio are 14 percent of teacher salaries, or $6,927 for a consulting teacher being paid $49,479 (the average salary, including the $5,000 stipend, for consulting teachers in 1997–98). In Toledo, the salaries paid to consulting teachers include the stipends the teachers would have received for directing extracurricular activities, even though the consulting teachers do not direct these activities during their service as consulting teachers. This adds to the pension costs as well. Inasmuch as teacher pensions are based upon a percentage of ones's salary during one's last three years of employment, some teachers try to serve as consulting teachers just before retirement in order to increase their pensions. In the past, the TFT discouraged this practice on the assumption that increasing one's pension was not the most desirable motivation for service as a consulting teacher. As a rough estimate, however, it appears that one in four of the consulting teachers served at least part of their three years in the three years preceding retirement. Obviously, any increases in the salary schedule will also add to the pension costs of peer review. In view of the tendency of pension costs to escalate when not closely monitored, districts considering peer review plans should review the issue carefully.

Due to an unusually high number of retirements, the Toledo school system employed 260 new teachers in 1997–98. One part-time and twenty full-time consulting teachers were appointed to supervise the interns. The average salary of the full-time consulting teachers was $49,479. The total cost per consulting teacher was as follows:

Average salary and benefits (Includes $5,000 stipend)	$49,479
Retirement (The Toledo public school system contributes 14 percent of salary to the Ohio State Teacher Retirement System)	$6,927
Insurance costs	$4,900
Workers compensation (2 percent of salary)	$990
Total per consulting teacher	$62,296

The $62,296 figure does not include various leave benefits, severance pay, tuition reimbursement, and other benefits that go to some but not all teachers; for this reason, $63,000 is a conservative estimate of the district cost for salaries and benefits per consulting teacher. Because an unusually high number of consulting teachers were utilized in 1997–98, the average salary was less than if a normal complement of consulting teachers were employed. Still, to be conservative, we can estimate that the average salary plus benefits per consulting teacher was $63,000 in 1997–98.

Mileage for Consulting Teachers

The consulting teachers in the Toledo plan occupy office space in a designated site, but do not receive secretarial assistance. However, because they travel from school to school, they are reimbursed for their mileage. This comes to about $700 per consulting teacher for the school year.

Administrator Costs

Administrator costs are based largely on the time administrators devote to peer review. In Columbus, there are three administrators on the governing board; in Toledo, four serve on the board. Inasmuch as we are tracking the consulting teacher costs in Toledo, we should also track the administrator costs there.

Administrator service on the Board of Review is a major component of administrator costs. The board meets for one full week in January, one full week in April after the second evaluation of the interns, one day in August, and one day about three weeks into the school year. Appeals may require up to two additional days of meetings. When the time required to prepare for and follow up on meetings is factored in, peer review in Toledo appears to require about one-tenth of the administrator work year of 232 days. The salaries and fringe benefits of the administrative members of the Board of Review average $84,027 a year; the cost per administrator of time devoted to peer review is $8,403. Thus, the cost for the four members on the Board of Review would be $33,612. The costs of secretarial/clerical time and office expenses must also be added to this figure. Overall, $50,000 appears to be a reasonable estimate of the costs of administrative time devoted to peer review in Toledo. Note, however, that the administrative costs are divided among all the interns as well as the teachers subject to intervention. Although there is no prescribed amount of time for intervention cases, there are so few of them that intervention cases do not materially change the estimates of costs per teacher subject to peer review.

Except in special cases, the consulting teachers in Toledo do not observe or evaluate new teachers in their second year; this is completely a school administration responsibility. Nevertheless, inasmuch as principals normally supervise only a few new teachers every year, the shift from peer review to administrative evaluation after the interns' first year of employment does not increase the workload of individual principals over what it would be under conventional procedures.

After the two-year probationary period in Toledo, teachers are normally offered a four-year renewable contract. The teachers must be evaluated at least once before the contract is renewed. This evaluation is an administration responsibility. If the administration does not recommend a four-year contract, the teachers are offered one-year contracts and are evaluated each year until awarded a four-year contract or terminated. The administration refers unsatisfactory evaluations to the Board of Review, which may assign a consulting teacher to work with the teacher under review. If both the administrator and the consulting teacher submit negative evaluations, the Board of Review may recommend intervention or nonrenewal.

In Toledo, teachers on continuing contract are normally not evaluated; in 1997–98, 41 percent of the Toledo teachers were not evaluated. This policy raises an interesting issue, to wit, the value of formally evaluating tenured teachers. The issue is not whether such teachers are sometimes incompetent; obviously, sometimes they are or have become incompetent. The issue is whether formal evaluations are necessary to identify such teachers. It may be that the principal or school administration is usually alerted to the situation through other means, so that formal observations and evaluations are not usually the basis for pursuing the matter. Formal observations and evaluations may not be necessary to identify incompetent teachers, although they may be required to terminate them.

It is doubtful whether most districts would or could agree not to evaluate teachers under continuing contracts; the political repercussions, especially after any egregious cases of teacher incompetence, would render it difficult to maintain such a policy. Significantly, restoration of evaluation of tenured teachers was a Toledo school district priority in 1997 negotiations; the district and the TFT bargained to impasse over the issue when the TFT would not agree to the restoration of evaluation by principals as well as by consulting teachers. Furthermore, the unions themselves have emphasized that the main purpose of evaluation should be professional improvement. If this is the case, why should teachers not be evaluated annually? In my opinion, annual evaluations of all tenured teachers are probably unnecessary, but the policy in Toledo, where (as I've noted) 41 percent of all teachers are never evaluated, and where the administration must obtain the union's permission to evaluate tenured teachers, is even less defensible. When the administration evaluates teachers, the union contends that the purpose of evaluation should be professional improvement and only minimal time should be devoted to teacher evaluation. When consulting teachers appointed by the union are paid a stipend to conduct the evaluations, the unions contend that a great deal of time is required to help teachers and make defensible decisions on renewal of employment. The union inconsistency is not necessarily an argument against the desirability of peer review as opposed to evaluation by administrators, but it does suggest a major short-term loss of union credibility.

In any event, on the basis of the preceding rough calculations, the Toledo district was spending about $5,200 per teacher subject to peer review in 1997–98. This estimate does not include legal and litigation costs that are not necessarily recurring but that may be substantial from time to time. It also does not include several overhead costs such as the costs of manuals for interns and consulting teachers. However, the direct costs per intern will rise to about $7,500 if the nine-to-one intern/consulting teacher ratio is restored.

Like other peer review districts, the Columbus district does not maintain a comprehensive account of the costs of peer review. CEA president John Grossman has conceded that the program is "expensive," but has not provided a breakdown of the costs.[3] Although most peer review costs in Columbus are at least as high as in Toledo, the costs per intern are probably less in Columbus because its consulting teachers are normally assigned eighteen interns compared to only nine in Toledo.

Cost Savings under Peer Review

Needless to say, any fiscal analysis of peer review should take into account any savings that result from the program. We must, however, distinguish between the savings that are built into a peer review program and the savings that allegedly result from the program. For instance, suppose a school district replaces teacher of mathematics A, who is paid $25,000 a year, with teacher B, who is paid $35,000 a year. There is an additional expenditure of $10,000, but there may be cost savings as well. B may be able to teach calculus, thereby rendering it unnecessary to employ anyone else to teach calculus. B may reduce the number of students taking remedial mathematics courses. The point is that some costs and savings are inherent in the change; others depend on the results of the change, and hence cannot be ascertained without evaluating the results. Our first task is to assess the costs and savings inherent in the structure of peer review; after that, we shall assess the savings or benefits that result or allegedly result from peer review.

The cost savings under peer review are mainly the principals' time that is required under conventional programs but not under peer review. This saving occurs during a teacher's first year of employment. Prior to peer review, Toledo principals were responsible for observing and evaluating new teachers. On the average, each principal evaluated two to three new teachers annually. Although some schools experience more turnover than others, the principals probably save three to five days annually because they no longer have to observe, evaluate, confer with, and write up classroom observations and evaluations of first-year teachers. The average salary plus benefits for Toledo principals in 1997–98 was $72,941, about $320 a day based on 227 working days. Their workloads relating to new teachers would vary widely in the absence of peer review. If principals devoted the equivalent of one and a half days to observing, evaluating, and conferring with each new teacher, the time saved as a result of peer review would be worth about $480 per new teacher. The amount is debatable, but the program relieves principals of a task they are otherwise required to perform. Nevertheless, it is interesting that most Toledo principals prefer a restoration of their rights to observe and evaluate new as well as tenured teachers.

Another time-savings issue in Toledo relates to the fact that the principals no longer evaluate teachers under continuing contract. Note, however, that this saving could be effectuated in the absence of peer review; school districts and unions that do not adopt peer review—indeed, that are adamantly opposed to it—might nevertheless dispense with systematic evaluation of tenured teachers. In fact, many teacher union contracts limit such evaluations virtually to the point of eliminating them. For these reasons, the time saved this way is not necessarily a saving due to peer review; if it is so categorized, there will be substantial variation in the time saved this way.

To be sure, contrary arguments can be made. One is that the elimination of evaluations of tenured teachers was part of an entire package. That is, it might be argued that this concession to the union was necessary to achieve its approval of peer review per se. The other argument is that as a result of peer review, principals need not observe and evaluate tenured teachers. This argument is difficult to accept because, at most, there is only a small difference in the identity of teachers who are awarded tenure under peer review and those awarded tenure under conventional arrangements. Furthermore, we have no way of knowing whether the differences redound to the superiority of peer review or of conventional procedures.

If one regards the time saved by not evaluating tenured teachers as due to peer review, difficult questions remain. How much time did principals devote to observing and evaluating teachers under continuing contract prior to peer review? No doubt there were large variations from school to school and from year to year, but there is no reliable data on the issue relating to the time before peer review was introduced. Evidence on the time principals in other districts devote to evaluating tenured teachers would be suggestive but not dispositive.

Peer review may well result in less litigation costs, especially costs associated with cases involving tenured teachers. In fact, although no data were offered on the issue, CEA president Grossman asserted that the Columbus school administration supported the peer review program mainly because of the savings in litigation costs. In any event, districts considering peer review should also consider other, less expensive ways to reduce their expenses related to litigation over teacher tenure. For example, sloppy observations and evaluations by administrators may be remediable in the absence of peer review.

One feature of the Columbus program illustrates the difficulty of accounting for all the costs of peer review. In Columbus, interns are allowed to enroll in two courses at Ohio State University (OSU). Neither the interns nor the school district pays for the courses, the costs of which are absorbed by the university. The faculty for these courses includes both consulting teachers and OSU faculty; hence, the costs to taxpayers are partly accounted for in the costs of the consulting teachers. Nevertheless, this "intern support program" is a real additional cost to taxpayers, although it does not show up in the school district budget. In addition, the Ohio Department of Education has set aside funds to evaluate peer review programs, and to facilitate their adoption throughout the state. Significantly, the University of Toledo received a grant of $116,000 in 1997 to prepare a packet of materials for districts interested in initiating peer review; there was no plan to include a discussion of the costs in the packet when I inquired about this in mid-December 1997.

Despite the lack of data, peer review unquestionably costs much more than conventional procedures. Because the additional costs go largely to teachers, and principals have more time to do other tasks, the additional costs required have avoided careful scrutiny thus far, but that is likely to change.

The fact that peer review costs more than conventional procedures is not necessarily a reason to reject it. The question is whether any additional benefits are worth the additional costs. Supporters of peer review claim the following benefits from it:

- More accurate identification of teachers who should not remain in the profession.
- Career-saving assistance to new teachers who would leave teaching if it were not for the help they received from the peer review program.
- A more collaborative spirit between the union and the administration.
- Higher teacher morale as a result of the stipends for consulting teachers and the utilization of teacher expertise.
- More time for principals to perform the tasks that they are better equipped and situated to perform.
- A decrease in litigation, or in the threat of litigation, over termination of teachers.

The following observations seem warranted.

- As a practical matter, it is virtually impossible to quantify many of the costs and benefits of peer review. This means that interests are likely to play a major role in its acceptance or rejection. These interests include greatly enhanced power of the teacher union, the teacher interest in receiving a substantial stipend for three years, and a school-board interest in defending a practice that it has accepted without rigorous analysis.
- The additional costs are much easier to demonstrate than the savings or benefits that allegedly result therefrom.
- The absence of a comprehensive summary of the costs of peer review is an especially troublesome fact.
- Although some of the benefits are plausible, they lack the kind of research support that should be required if they are to be accepted.

The teacher unions' neglect of the costs of peer review illustrates a significant but much neglected contrast to the unions' attitudes toward changes they oppose. For example, when the unions oppose contracting out, they demand extensive research on every aspect of the matter; it is generally impossible to satisfy their research demands when the unions oppose a practice or a reform initiative. Reforms opposed by the unions are "fads and frills," "quick fixes," or some other pejorative that connotes failure to analyze the reform carefully. Let the "reform" be one advocated by the teacher unions, and their level of scrutiny declines precipitously.

7

Peer Review in Other Contexts

In its long history, the NEA has reversed its policies several times. There is nothing objectionable in doing so; any open-minded individual or organization will change its views from time to time. Nevertheless, perhaps the most astonishing feature of the new unionism is the NEA's unstinting praise for labor/management relations at the General Motors Saturn plant in Spring Hill, Tennessee. The NEA even subsidizes travel to the plant for school officials to allow them to observe a working model of labor/management relations that supposedly deserves emulation in education. The AFT has also cited the Saturn plant as a model for public education.

The AFT, however, was never concerned about the question of whether the "industrial model" is applicable as a guide for education. Indeed, for much of its history, the AFT took pride in its alleged similarity to industrial unions. In contrast, during the 1960s and 1970s, when NEA/AFT competition was very intense, the NEA constantly asserted that the "industrial model" was not applicable to public education. In fact, there is no such entity as the "industrial model"; collective bargaining in the private sector is very different from industry to industry and from company to company. Even the unions of professional baseball, football, and basketball players show remarkable differences as well as similarities, so perhaps we should say that there are hundreds of "industrial models."

In any event, the teacher unions are vigorously promoting labor relations at the Saturn plant as a model for public education. The spin is that the union and management there have laid aside their former adversarial relationships and now act as partners in promoting a better car at a lower price.

Labor/management relations at the Saturn plant are governed by a "Memorandum of Agreement" that does not include many of the detailed rules governing hours, workload, transfers, assignments, job descriptions, and other topics usually included in United Auto Workers (UAW) contracts. Obviously, if such cooperative relationships could be adopted in public education, it would be an enormous step forward. It all seems too good to be true, and, unfortunately, it is insofar as public education is concerned.

In the first place, the basic incentives that motivate the union and the auto workers at Saturn do not prevail in public education. Every automobile worker knows that the threat to his job is not from management. It is from other carmakers. Management can show workers what cars its competitors are making and at what price they are being sold—and can be credible in stating that "If we can't do better, we are out of business." In this connection, note the following references to competition in the Saturn Memorandum of Agreement:

> *1. Preamble:* Since GM and the Union first met and authorized the establishment of a study center and the creation of the Corporation, the parties recognize that the global *competitiveness* in the auto industry has significantly increased. GM and the Union further recognize the necessity of further developing this innovative approach to Union/Management relations and the necessary staffing to accomplish our mutual objectives. General Motors, Saturn Corporation and the Union understand fully the necessity to successfully forge a renewed commitment to a cooperative problem solving relationship and demonstrate that a *competitive,* world class, quality vehicle will be developed and manufactured in the United States with a represented work force.

> *9. Symbols:* To the degree possible, recognizing the need to remain *competitive,* consistency of treatment for everyone (represented and non-represented) will be an important objective for Saturn.

> *16. Training:* The success of Saturn in meeting its mission in an internationally *competitive* environment is dependent upon the continuous development and implementation of new tools, methods and cutting edge technology.

> *17. Job Design:* In keeping with the Saturn mission and culture, each Work Unit will have the responsibility and authority to produce quality products to schedule at *competitive* costs. The Units will have responsibility for both direct and indirect work, including training, housekeeping, provision for relief, etc. Individual jobs will be designed with the appropriate resources to develop the optimum balance between people and technology, taking into account health, safety and ergonomic issues, with ongoing responsibility to determine methods to become more *competitive.*

32. Components Manufacturing: . . . [T]he parties agree to review the specifics of the component part(s) being considered to determine if Saturn can be *competitive* in quality and cost.

Dec. 13, 1994 Letter from [UAW Vice President] Stephen Yokich to [Saturn President] Richard LeFauve: The parties recognize that the Corporation is marketing vehicles in a highly *competitive* market. As such, the job security of Saturn members is defined by the success that Saturn achieves within this market.[1]

In discussions I have had with UAW officials from the Saturn plant, they have been emphatic in stating that the UAW and its members at Saturn would not have accepted the changes embodied in the Memorandum of Agreement in the absence of competition. Competition, however, is precisely what the NEA and the AFT are trying desperately to avoid. They are well aware of the fact that private-sector union membership has declined from 36 percent of the private-sector labor force in the 1950s to only 11 percent today—and is still going down. Without a doubt, the highest priority of the teacher unions is to maintain the public school monopoly. As long as their efforts are successful, there is little likelihood that teachers and their unions will have the incentives to increase educational productivity. It is wishful thinking to expect that generalized appeals to the welfare of children or "professionalism" or public opinion will persuade teachers and their unions to adopt basic changes in their modus operandi.

An example may help to clarify the problem. For years, the teacher unions have tried to relieve teachers from "nonprofessional" duties, such as monitoring school cafeterias, making sure children get on school buses, and collecting money from students for school activities. The union argument was that teachers would be more productive if they were not saddled with these "nonprofessional" tasks. Supposedly, if everyone performed the tasks appropriate to his or her skill level, education would be more productive. Furthermore, the unions have done their utmost to restrict the use of part-time employees, especially those who are not given fringe benefits (or a pro rata share of them).

These union-driven rules have a negative effect upon educational productivity; they drive up costs without any increase in efficiency, or any improvement in educational outcomes. In the first place, the union position is based upon a widespread fallacy, to wit, that the skill or "professional" dimension of teachers' work is teaching. Sometimes it is, sometimes it is not. An analogy may help to clarify this point. When a physician treats a patient, the highest skill level required may be diagnosis. Once an accurate diagnosis is made, treatment may be as simple as providing the patient with pills that the patient can take without any help from anyone. In other situations, diagnosis is simple, but treatment requires a high degree of skill and knowledge. It may be very obvious that the patient has a fractured skull, but treatment may be an extremely complex, demanding task.

The point of the example applies fully to education. In some situations, diagnosing why a student is not learning may be the "professional" task; drills that can be provided by teacher aides or family members may be the appropriate solution. In other situations, the diagnosis may be obvious but the instructional remedy may require a high level of skill and knowledge. Widespread though it is, the notion that teaching, that is, providing instruction, is the "professional" work is a fallacy.

Another fallacy has even more harmful consequences. Let us grant that different tasks require different levels of skill and knowledge and that, generally speaking, it is desirable to avoid having teachers work at below their skill level. Nevertheless, what is true generally is often not true in particular circumstances. Technicians can measure blood pressure or subject blood samples to various tests. Nevertheless, it would be absurd to prohibit doctors from performing these tasks because an M.D. is not required to perform them adequately. In countless situations, the most cost-effective use of resources requires individuals to perform tasks that can be done by less skilled individuals.

For three decades, the teacher unions have been aggressively promoting a variety of restrictions on educational productivity. In many districts, they have successfully negotiated restrictions that teachers like, even if the restrictions had a negative effect on the efficiency of district operations as a whole. Increases in educational productivity will require more than a change in union thinking, although that in itself will be a formidable task. Union officers and staff have devoted enormous resources to achieving objectives that must now be repudiated if educational productivity is to be the highest union priority; the entire culture of teacher unionism would have to change. The incentives required to make such a change possible do not exist in public education. And if the NEA and the AFT have their way, the necessary incentives will never exist there.

The Applicability of the Saturn Model to Education

To appreciate the problems facing a teacher union that tries to adopt the Saturn model, it is essential to recognize the contractual implications of the model. Figure 7.1 is a reproduction of the index to the contract between the CEA and the Columbus Board of Education. Needless to say, most of the items under these headings have been portrayed as union "victories." Is it realistic to expect the CEA to drop these contractual benefits to improve education?

Figure 7.1. Index to Agreement between the Columbus Board of Education and the Columbus Education Association[2]

CHAPTER 100
101 - RECOGNITION
102 - RESPONSIBILITY OF THE BOARD
103 - AUTHORITY OF THE SUPERINTENDENT
104 - RESPONSIBILITY OF THE ASSOCIATION
105 - EQUAL EMPLOYMENT RIGHTS
106 - CONTINUOUS PERFORMANCE PLEDGE
107 - PRESENT POLICIES
108 - BOARD-ASSOCIATION CONSULTATION
109 - RIGHTS OF THE ASSOCIATION
110 - GRIEVANCE PROCEDURE
111 - ARBITRATION
112 - AGENCY FEE

CHAPTER 200
201 - ACADEMIC FREEDOM
202 - ASSOCIATION BUILDING COUNCIL
203 - ELECTION OF DEPARTMENT CHAIRPERSONS
204 - LENGTH OF SCHOOL DAY
205 - BUILDING STAFF MEETINGS
206 - TEACHING ENVIRONMENT AND NEW BUILDINGS
207 - GUIDELINES FOR CLASSROOM VISITATIONS AND TEACHER
      CONFERENCES
208 - CLASSROOM ATMOSPHERE
209 - CO-CURRICULAR ACTIVITIES AND EXTRA DUTIES
210 - TEACHER-PARENT CONFERENCES AND REPORTS TO
      PARENTS
211 - ASSIGNMENTS AND TRANSFERS
212 - RESIDENCE

CHAPTER 300
301 - CLASS SIZE
302 - TEACHER CLASS LOAD
303 - ABILITY GROUPING
304 - STUDY HALLS
305 - SPECIAL EDUCATION
306 - FOREIGN LANGUAGE
307 - ELEMENTARY ART, VOCAL MUSIC, AND PHYSICAL
      EDUCATION PROGRAMS

CHAPTER 400
401 - TEACHER EVALUATION
402 - TEACHER CONTRACT FORMS
403 - PROFESSIONAL PERSONNEL RECORDS
404 - PROFESSIONAL BEHAVIOR

CHAPTER 500
501 - ANNUAL EVALUATION
502 - LIBRARIES
503 - ALTERNATIVE SCHOOLS
504 - TEACHING AIDS
505 - INTEGRATED TEXTBOOKS
506 - COMMITTEE PROCEDURES

CHAPTER 600
601 - EDUCATIONAL AIDES
602 - VOLUNTEER WORKERS
603 - SCHOOL COUNSELORS
604 - SCHOOL NURSES
605 - SCHOOL NURSE ORIENTATION AND IN-SERVICE
606 - SCHOOL SOCIAL WORKERS
607 - KINDERGARTEN TEACHERS

CHAPTER 700
701 - SICK LEAVE
702 - LEAVES OF ABSENCE
703 - SABBATICAL LEAVE
704 - REDUCTIONS IN PERSONNEL

CHAPTER 800
801 - SUMMER EMPLOYMENT
802 - USE OF COLLEGE SCRIP
803 - PHYSICAL EXAMINATION
804 - ANNUITY PROGRAMS
805 - DISABILITY INSURANCE PAYROLL DEDUCTIONS
806 - HOSPITAL, SURGICAL, AND MAJOR MEDICAL INSURANCE
807 - DENTAL INSURANCE
808 - VISION CARE INSURANCE
809 - TERM LIFE INSURANCE
810 - SEVERANCE PAY
811 - VOLUNTARY EMPLOYEE SEPARATION ASSISTANCE PLAN

One would hardly think so, since the benefits were supposed to result in a stable, highly motivated staff. And if the CEA were to waive these contractual benefits, who would establish rules to govern the issues in the absence of a contract? What rules would be established? Would the extent of the benefits be left up to scores of schools or work teams throughout the district?

One of the outcomes of collective bargaining has been its tendency to clarify rights and responsibilities at the workplace. In education, however, the Saturn model would have the opposite effect. In both education and carmaking, it is essential to clarify employee obligations and benefits; even the Saturn Memorandum of Agreement, brief as it is by industry standards, goes a long way toward resolving compensation issues for everyone in the bargaining unit. When it comes to the work arrangements, however, the Saturn model will crash immediately in public schools. In manufacturing cars, there is widespread agreement on the product or on the trade-offs at the workplace. Everyone recognizes that mileage economy, safety, and passenger comfort are desirable; the trade-offs between these objectives are settled at a much higher level than the factory floor. For the most part, flexibility at the worksite is essential only to develop the most productive way to achieve commonly understood and accepted objectives. Education, however, is characterized by multiple, often conflicting goals, and the trade-offs are not clear. It is unrealistic to expect agreement on the means at the school level—the equivalent of the shop floor in carmaking—when there is so little agreement on the ends, or the priorities among the ends to be achieved. Furthermore, the Saturn work units (generally made up of six to fifteen members) have clearly defined responsibilities and bring specific skills to their responsibilities. No one has even suggested how such a restructuring of public education could function, and the institutional obstacles, such as teacher training, school architecture, and political instead of corporate leadership, are formidable indeed.

There is an even more compelling reason why the Saturn model would not be appropriate in public education. The UAW/Saturn Memorandum of Agreement does not include most of the union restrictions on utilization of the workforce. In return, however, the union is supposedly treated as an equal partner in most phases of plant operation.

As one NEA publication commented:

> Significantly, the contract contains no management-rights clause. The employees are full partners in the operation. Everyone has an equal share of responsibility and accountability in all decision-making—from strategic planning to day-to-day problem-solving.
>
> Too good to be true? Not if you work at Saturn or were one of the group of NEA leaders and staff who recently toured the Saturn automobile plant in Spring Hill, Tennessee.
>
> The NEA folks met with Saturn management and the United Auto Workers local to discuss how Saturn's distinctive labor-management arrangement might be applied to education. NEA President Bob Chase said he hopes the NEA can use some of the lessons learned from the Saturn-UAW team concept.[3]

When I asked a UAW official whether this arrangement would be feasible in public education, his answer was an unhesitating "yes." I asked for an example, and the reply was "the curriculum." This reply illustrates why the Saturn model is not applicable to public education.

It is one thing for a private employer to bring in such "partners" as the employer deems appropriate. For a school board to treat the teacher union as a full partner may be appealing rhetoric, but it is atrocious public policy; it is indefensible to give one special interest such a privileged position in the enactment of public policy.

Furthermore, there is no accountability for the union as a "partner" in the public school situation. Suppose the school board and the union agree on a wide range of matters—curriculum, testing, grading policy, and so on. And suppose also, as will happen on occasion, that the jointly adopted policies turn out to be disastrous. Presumably, the public can replace the school board, but it has no control whatsoever over the union personnel or the union members. The public cannot vote the union leadership out of office; nor can it dismiss any teachers for supporting or endorsing the disastrous policies. In short, the Saturn model, if applied to education, would provide the union with a veto power over public policy but no accountability for the results. In the Saturn situation, the mistakes show up in the marketplace; but taxpayers and students, not the teacher unions, would pay for comparable mistakes in public education. It is interesting that the teacher unions, ever so alert to prevent public funds from being spent without public accountability, should promote policies that guarantee this outcome.

The Saturn plant was a new facility. Many workers at the plant had not been employed previously, and hence were not the beneficiaries of preexisting UAW contracts that included various restrictions on productivity. The situation in school districts will be very different; teachers will be urged to give up rights and benefits they have struggled for years to achieve. To say the least, it will not be easy to persuade them to do so.

Realistically, it will be more difficult to effectuate a basic change in the culture of public education than it is in the private sector. Prospective teachers are trained in teacher education programs that do not discuss or even envisage competition in the education industry. Furthermore, they rarely if ever are required to consider their role as members of an occupational group, that is, their role in a union or professional organization. Such attention as is paid to these matters is promotional and superficial, not analytic. The neglect of the teachers' role as occupational citizens is not confined to teacher education; despite the importance of occupational citizenship, our educational system pays little or no attention to it.

One might suppose that competition for students among institutions of higher education would have led to a more realistic understanding of competition in colleges of education, but this is not the case. Institutions of higher education compete by giving higher grades, easier courses, and minimal requirements for degrees and teaching certificates. The reason is simple and in no way negates the case for a competitive education industry. There is no systematic comparison or evaluation of teachers on the basis of where they received their formal training. It is impossible to link teaching performance to institutions of higher education in any systematic way. This being the case, there is great pressure on institutions that train teachers to compete on the basis of easier programs. In other fields, this is not the case, or is much less the case. Consumers can evaluate automobiles on objective criteria such as safety features or miles per gallon. In a competitive K–12 education industry, objective criteria would emerge over time if they were not immediately available. The point here, however, is that the required changes in the teacher culture to make educational achievement the highest priority are even more daunting than has been previously indicated.

Finally, any effort to adopt or adapt the Saturn model to public education is likely to face insuperable legal and policy problems. In the private sector, the subjects of bargaining are categorized as follows:

- *Mandatory*. Employers and unions must bargain on these subjects if requested to do so by the other party.
- *Permissive*. The parties are not required to bargain on permissive subjects but may do so if they wish.

• *Prohibited.* The parties may not bargain on these matters; for example, a proposal to pay union members more than nonunion employees.

At the Saturn plant, the management agreed to negotiate on a wide range of subjects in the "permissive" category. It is difficult to see why school boards should do so. Generally speaking, it is in management's interest to limit the scope of bargaining, not expand it. If a matter is not subject to bargaining, management can act unilaterally with respect to it. It is difficult to see why school management should or would voluntarily limit its freedom to act on a host of important issues in exchange for the vague benefits of "partnership" with the union. Even if school management was inclined to do so, the more issues that it negotiates with the union, the fewer the issues that are resolved by school boards through normal democratic processes. In any event, if consulting teachers are not to be regarded as supervisors, and if peer review plans are not to violate the duty of fair representation, many of the state bargaining statutes will have to be amended in various ways. Despite the political power of the state teacher unions, legislative approval of these amendments cannot be assumed. In fact, such amendments may not be proposed for many years to come, if at all, by the state teacher unions opposed to peer review.

Peer Review in Higher Education

Peer review is a very common practice in higher education—so much so that it is surprising that the teacher unions have not cited it more often. Perhaps one reason is that Dal Lawrence, the moving spirit behind the Toledo program, was determined that the participants would never ask university professors for assistance.[4] In contrast, the Columbus program explicitly states that it is a joint effort by the Columbus Education Association, the Columbus school district, and Ohio State University.

Although the basic rationale is the same, peer review in higher education usually differs from the practice in K–12 education in the following ways:

1. The peer reviewers in higher education are not released from their normal duties to serve as peer reviewers. Service as a peer reviewer is usually part of the service tenured professors are supposed to provide along with teaching and research. In some instances, professors secure load credit for such service, but it is never a full-time assignment.

2. There are seldom any institutional limits on how long academics serve as peer reviewers.

3. Peer review in higher education usually focuses on the candidate's research. The assumption is that only other academics, especially in the same field, are able to evaluate the research in their field. In many institutions, especially when tenure and promotion decisions are at stake, peer review includes outside reviewers who are paid to submit evaluations of the candidate's research.

4. The deliberations of the peer reviewers are much less accessible to the individuals subjected to peer review. In fact, this issue has led to litigation, especially in cases in which a candidate for tenure alleges racial or gender or religious discrimination. In this respect, peer review in K–12 education is a much more open and defensible practice.

5. Peer review in higher education is not ordinarily governed by contractual provisions between a union and an institution of higher education. First, a much lower proportion of professors work pursuant to a collective bargaining contract. Second, legally, peer review is often cited as a reason to avoid unionization. As a matter of fact, academics who participate in a peer review program may thereby lose the right to unionize, on the grounds that the peer reviewers are performing what are essentially management functions. In *NLRB v. Yeshiva University* (1980), the U.S. Supreme Court held that a university faculty as a whole was not entitled to the protections accorded to employees under federal labor laws because the faculty collectively made management decisions.[5]

6. Peer review is less often utilized in higher education to make termination decisions affecting tenured professors.

7. Peer review in higher education tends to be part of a system of faculty self-government that covers a much broader range of issues than peer review in K–12 education. In higher education, peer review is frequently part of governance in which the faculty decides the grading system, faculty load, course and degree requirements, and a host of other governance issues.

8. Peer review in higher education is often utilized as an editorial policy in professional journals. Authors submit articles that are then farmed out to "peers" for their opinions on the professional worthiness of the articles. Professional journals that follow this practice usually have more prestige than journals that do not.

Notwithstanding its widespread, taken-for-granted status, peer review in higher education is subject to the same criticisms that I have made of peer review in K–12 education. The professors who serve on peer review committees that make effective recommendations on tenure are performing managerial functions without management responsibilities; one rarely, if ever, encounters a professor who experienced any adverse consequences as a result of deficient performance as a peer reviewer. Surely, not all academics make the right recommendations all the time. In higher education even more than in K–12, academics do not make decisions because they are right; the decisions are sup-posedly right because they are made by professors.

Whether or not the reader agrees with this criticism, the origins and context of peer review in higher education differ drastically from its emergence in K–12, and the support for peer review in K–12 education has not relied upon the practice in higher education. For these reasons, a detailed analysis of peer review in higher education is not necessary here. Readers who wish to pursue the topic may find discussions of it elsewhere to be helpful.[6]

8

The Union Stake in Peer Review

In analyzing peer review, one is reminded that men find it easy to convert their interests into principles. Assume that a district is spending $100,000 annually to evaluate and assist new teachers. Assume also that this amount must be drastically increased to provide adequate time for observation, assistance, and evaluation. What plan would most teachers prefer—one in which the district increases its budget for administrative evaluators, resulting in more administrators in more teachers' classrooms? Or a plan whereby a large number of teachers who must be approved by the union will receive a substantial stipend for three years while evaluating new teachers—work that is more attractive than classroom teaching for most teachers?

On the record, the literature on peer review ignores the self-interest of consulting teachers and their unions. These senior teachers are usually a dominant force, if not the controlling one, in the teacher unions, just as are the senior members of unions in other fields. If the literature on peer review had confronted this issue in a realistic way, one might have more confidence in the case for peer review. As matters stand, however, the unions indignantly decry the efforts to portray teachers as money-hungry pedagogues who care only about their paychecks. As erroneous as this would be, it is not more so than the portrayal of teachers as totally unaffected by the compensation issues in peer review. We must also consider the union stake in peer review. As will be evident, the union stake overlaps with the teacher stake, but is far from identical with it.

Peer Review and Union Control

A realistic evaluation of peer review plans must recognize that they greatly strengthen a union's control over its members, especially potential dissidents. First, the union exercises a veto power over the selection of consulting teachers. Overt opposition to the union is reduced because such opposition may jeopardize one's prospects for tenure or for appointment as a consulting teacher. Even if the union members of the Board of Review evaluate candidates solely on the basis of their professional performance, the candidates themselves will often fear that the union members of the Board of Review will evaluate nonunion or antiunion candidates more harshly.

Indeed, the fact that the consulting teachers must be recommended by their building representatives is another troubling feature of the most prominent peer review plans. The building representatives are not appointed or elected because of superior insight into teaching. Their functions are to hold union meetings at the schools, receive and process grievances, keep members informed about union activities, and convey teacher views to the leadership echelons of the union. Again, regardless of the purity of individual motives, there is a coercive element in the situation. Furthermore, the potential dissident lacks the resources to oppose the union in these situations.

Interestingly enough, the teacher unions have opposed merit pay on the grounds that it would be utilized to reward antiunion teachers. Can we assume that a plan controlled in large part by the union, or, minimally, subject to its veto power, will show no animus against antiunion teachers? The assumption that school administrators are biased against union activists, but union activists are not biased against antiunion teachers, may appeal to union members, but it is hardly persuasive.

It is easy to visualize NEA/AFT reactions to the foregoing criticisms. Since they have invested a great deal in portraying peer review as a major step toward educational improvement, a new role for unions, and union assumption of professional status, it is very unlikely that the unions will publicly acknowledge any merit in the foregoing criticisms. Privately, some will; some already have. The official line, though, is likely to be as follows: First, we were criticized for being overly protective of incompetent teachers. Now, we are being criticized for union efforts to help beginning teachers or guide them out of the profession. No matter what we do, we can't satisfy right-wing extremists who are determined to destroy public education.

Aside from the fact that such a response does not address the specific criticisms set forth here, consider this paradox: Most citizens have a negative view of unions. At the same time, most have a favorable attitude toward the NEA. The explanation is not that the NEA is considered to be "a good union." It is that the NEA is not perceived as a union at all. If it were, its prestige would experience a substantial decline. One can argue about the proportion of citizens who have a negative view of unions, but there is no doubt that the NEA enjoys a much higher favorable rating than unions generally because the association is not widely perceived as a union.

The "new union" must, therefore, be understood in this context. When the UAW or Teamsters strike, no one doubts that the intended beneficiaries are auto workers and teamsters. When teachers strike, it is allegedly for the benefit of children. Teacher union success in promoting teacher welfare as pupil welfare is phenomenal. The taxpayer dilemma that arises is similar to the one that arises in efforts to discourage welfare mothers from bearing additional children. How can we encourage responsible adult behavior without hurting innocent children? For a time, the NEA took pride in a kind of in-your-face unionism to persuade teachers that the association was a tough union, not a weak imitation of the AFT. Here and there, one sees a residual of this pose, but the word is out: Down with any language that connotes "union"; up with anything that connotes pupil welfare or "profession." This is the strategic environment in which the new union was conceived and has emerged. If significant changes had really taken place, the fact that various pressures triggered them would not be important. The question is: What are the changes, in NEA/AFT personnel, budget, and policies, that are the result of the "new union" initiative? Whatever they are, they clearly do not involve significant changes in union personnel or budgets, or in the unions' program. Failure to raise this issue is a major deficiency in the media's treatment of the "new union."

The TFT Contract: Some Observations

Authorities on collective bargaining emphasize the importance of evaluating contractual provisions in the light of the entire contract. This caveat applies in two ways. First, the implications of any contractual provision may be crucially affected by other provisions. For example, a broad definition of "grievance" will be less troublesome if the grievance procedure does not culminate in binding arbitration; a narrower definition of "grievance" may be very troublesome in a contract with binding arbitration and brief time limits for management to respond.

A review of contractual provisions in the context of the entire contract is essential for another reason. Frequently, we want to know the philosophical or strategic orientation of the contract as a whole. Is it based on a strong management-rights perspective? Co-management by the union? Clearly defined trade-offs between these extremes? The entire contract often provides a context that affects evaluation of specific provisions. What light, if any, is shed upon peer review by a review of the entire contract in peer review districts?

Before responding to this question by reviewing the Toledo contract, some data on the Toledo school district will be helpful. In 1995, the Toledo school district:

- Served approximately 38,500 students, down from a high of 60,000 in the 1960s and 1970s.
- Operated forty-eight elementary, eight junior high (grades seven through eight), and eight high schools (grades nine through twelve).
- Employed 4,400 employees.
- Negotiated with unions representing nine different bargaining units. The TFT represents approximately 2,500 in the teacher unit, 360 in the substitute teacher unit, and 370 in the paraprofessional unit. The Toledo Association of Administrative Personnel (TAAP) represents 320 employees. There were five separate American Federation of State, County, and Municipal Employees (AFSCME) locals as follows:

    Local 249, custodians and hall monitors, 235 employees.
    Local 2174, clerical and technical employees, 375 employees.
    Local 272, building operations, skilled trades, 170 employees.
    Local 840, food service employees, 280 to 300 employees.
    Local 2853, transportation employees, 180 to 200 employees.
- Only fourteen district employees were not represented by a union in 1995.
- The total budget for the district was $220 million.

One issue raised by these data relates to the number of teachers required to operate a peer review program. Ideally, the consulting teachers teach the same grade level and subject as the interns; having teachers evaluate the subject-matter competence of teachers in different subjects and grade levels could lead to major problems, especially since subject-matter competence is an important criterion in the peer review process. Nevertheless, even in a district as large as Toledo, consulting teachers cannot always be recruited from the same grade level or subject being taught by the teachers subject to peer review.

Obviously, the smaller the district in terms of personnel, the more difficult it is to recruit consulting teachers with an appropriate background. For instance, suppose a district employs only one physics teacher who is about to retire. Even if the teacher met the criteria to be a consulting teacher, it would be prohibitively expensive for the teacher to mentor his or her replacement. The lack of mentoring experience and opportunity to work with other mentors would be a negative likely to lead to conflict one way or another. We cannot say that a district must employ a specified number of teachers to conduct a peer review program; we can say, however, that as the number of teachers employed by the district is reduced, more negatives emerge. At some point, which may differ from district to district, the negatives simply become prohibitive.

The upshot is to undermine further the claim that peer review is the way for teachers to raise standards for entry into teaching. The doctors, lawyers, and dentists who practice in small school districts have passed a state examination applicable to all parties in the state seeking to practice these professions. Even in the most optimistic scenario, peer review cannot function to prevent large numbers of teachers from being certified as regular teachers outside the peer review process.

For purposes of discussion, however, let us assume that there is no size-of-district problem. Nonetheless, the union/school district contracts in peer review districts strongly suggest that peer review emerges only in districts that allow the union to co-manage the district. In Toledo, the union exercises a de facto veto power over most educational policies as well as personnel functions. These are not only my conclusions, based on a study of the 224-page TFT contract; they are also the conclusions of knowledgeable authorities who conducted an intensive review of the TFT contract in conjunction with extensive interviews with school board members, administrators, and officers of the seven unions representing district employees. The study compared the TFT contract with the teacher contracts in Akron, Canton, Cincinnati, Cleveland, Columbus, Dayton, and Youngstown—all urban Ohio districts to which Toledo is often compared. The study director was R. Theodore Clark, Jr., one of the country's leading authorities on public-sector bargaining and a past president of the National Public Employer Labor Relations Association (NPELRA), the national organization of public employer representatives in labor negotiations. The study, which Clark coauthored with Robert C. Long, included the following comments under the heading of "Reasons for Optimism":

Talented and Experienced Union Leadership— . . . Presently, the school system appears to have union leaders with many years of experience, considerable credibility and strength, and the depth of vision and understanding to know that "business as usual" will not serve the long-term interests of their members nor is it the direction in which labor needs to move if labor wants to continue to play a significant role in the school system. . . .

Successful Examples of Labor Management Cooperation in the Toledo Public Schools— . . . Among the initiatives that labor and management both point to with some pride are the Intern and Intervention programs begun in 1981 with the TFT, a number of similar mentoring, evaluation, and management training programs initiated by TAAP, and the recent initiatives with site-based management schools.[1]

Despite these positive comments, the Long/Clark report is a devastating analysis of the collective bargaining agreements in the Toledo school district. Long and Clark summarize the "highlights" of their study that "have the greatest impact on student achievement and better use of taxpayer resources" as follows:

1. *Restrictive Management Rights Provisions*—The typical collective bargaining agreement with the Toledo Public School System has:
   * no management rights clause or one of little value;
   * broad provisions freezing all past practices and policies not referenced in the contract;
   * extremely broad definition of the term "grievance" such that issues going well beyond the scope of the collective bargaining agreement can be submitted to the grievance and arbitration procedure;
   * provisions restricting the right to subcontract, including a successors and assigns clause in the AFSCME contract;
   * vague or limiting provisions regarding management's right to lay off employees;
   * no provision terminating management's duty to bargain with the union during the term of the collective bargaining agreement (a so-called "zipper clause").
2. *Restrictions On Outside Recruitment*— . . . The TFT agreements are structured so that it is virtually impossible to obtain a regular full-time teaching position with the school district without first serving a period of time as a substitute teacher, thus effectively excluding from serious consideration applicants for teaching positions who are coming straight out of college or who are thinking of transferring from another school district, unless such applicants are willing to "wait their turn" in the substitute teacher apprenticeship route. . . . This shuts out most teachers who do not presently live in the Toledo area. . . .
3. *Job Assignments and Transfers Are Overly Dependent On Seniority*— Job assignments and transfers are dependent almost entirely on seniority considerations. . . . For example, the seniority-driven system creates a situation where it is possible that a high school may not be able to have a male physical education teacher. Similarly, it is often not possible to match up the particular schools' combined needs for teaching assignments and talents necessary for extracurricular programs of importance, whether they be debate, drama, athletics, or the like. . . . Similarly, when new innovative programs are devised, there is no way to ensure that the enthusiasts will be assigned to those programs, as they may not have the seniority to bid into those new opportunities. In addition, school principals have virtually no say in who the building secretary

will be, as those placements are driven by a seniority-based bidding system.

Even where the seniority-based assignment and transfer system places qualified candidates in logical positions, it does so often at the extraordinary expense of causing a domino reshuffling effect that includes a series of job bumping, vacancy and bidding cycles that can continue for months. . . . Based upon enrollment changes that may trigger a change in staffing levels, a whole series of job displacements can be unleashed, creating enormous inefficiency for a considerable period of time while employees exercise bumping rights to switch to new assignments at different schools for different supervisors. An example of this is the so-called "Bump Day" under the AFSCME secretarial contract unit where, during the first week of August each year, anywhere from 85 to 150 of the 375 members of that bargaining unit are reshuffled to new assignments.

4. . . . [I]t is our sense that the Toledo Public Schools pay unusually generous benefits to both full-time and part-time employees outside of the base wage schedule. Illustrative of these fringe benefits and off-schedule payments are the following: . . .

- Excessive time off provisions and loose controls on the use of many paid leaves, with the result of significant absenteeism problems in certain bargaining units.
- An extraordinary array of fringe benefits for part-time employees, including full benefits for those working 20 hours or more a week in many instances and partial benefits for those working fewer hours.
- The second highest workers' compensation claims rates of any school district in the state.
- Generous severance pay plan through the buyout of sick leave benefits upon termination of employment.
- Full compensation to all employees who do not work on "calamity" or "inclement weather" days, with the requirement that management pay twice for employees who work on such days. Moreover, if more than five such days are missed in a year, the school district is not only required to pay the employees to stay at home for those five days, but also to pay employees extra to make up a day to meet state attendance day requirements. Such an additional make-up day would cost the district approximately $1 million per day. . . .

6. *Inadequate Control Over Staffing Levels And Job Descriptions* — . . . While it is common for unions to have the right to negotiate over the effects of significant changes in the scope of job functions, the TPS [Toledo Public School] agreements appear to give unions a virtual veto over any proposed change in job functions and assignments.

7. *Principals Have Inadequate Authority And Responsibility* — The principal's job has been demeaned and trivialized by the collective bargaining agreements that govern innumerable management functions and decisions. Principals have minimal power and authority to direct the work of AFSCME employees at their buildings, and have little or no say about who works at their particular school, whether they be teachers, AFSCME employees or even their own secretary. . . . Principals have a minimal role in evaluating and mentoring teachers, and have little or no say in selecting the teachers who will work at their schools, except in the few site-based management schools where this entire situation is being changed. . . .

8. . . . There are inadequate means in the existing collective bargaining agreements to motivate and reward exceptional performance. . . .

9. *Collective Bargaining Agreements Are Unnecessarily Laden With Day-to-Day Trivia* — It is unnecessary to have provisions in collective bargaining agreements stating that the coffee pots in teacher lounges will have automatic shut-off switches, yet innumerable day-to-day matters like this have become the subject of collective bargaining and have been memorialized in contractual provisions. When day-to-day administrative details become commonplace in collective bargaining agreements, it invites individuals who would normally be held accountable for performance to throw up their hands and disclaim responsibility for what the system is producing or how it works, with the argument (often well-founded, unfortunately) that they simply don't have enough control. This process . . . also creates anomalous and probably unintended situations that are extremely frustrating to the individuals involved, such as an arrangement whereby a principal's work schedule is different than the work schedule of his or her secretary. . . .

10. . . . Many interviewees commented that the school day for students, teachers, principals and staff at the schools is too short and should be lengthened. This point was certainly borne out by our research which reveals that Toledo has by far the shortest workday of any of the school systems we studied. . . .

11. *The AFSCME Contract Is Burdened With Too Many Job Classifications* — The AFSCME contract has numerous job classifications that are now outdated and extinct, and the job classifications that are still relevant are almost certainly stratified into far too many gradations. . . . At times, for example, building principals are unable to find an AFSCME maintenance employee who has authority, within the scope of their job description, to perform such simple maintenance tasks as throwing salt on the parking lot during an ice storm. . . .

13. *There Is Inadequate Long-Term Consistent Strategic Planning For Collective Bargaining By Management* — ... [T]here are only 14 management employees of the school district who are not represented for purposes of collective bargaining. To make matters worse, their own compensation and benefit packages historically have been tied by the Board of Education to the outcome of collective bargaining agreements with the employee unions, thus creating an unnecessary conflict of interest. ...

14. ... The labor agreements as a whole are replete with obstacles to innovation and experimentation. There are few incentives for change and innovation — just barriers standing in the way. ...

   The foregoing is by no means an exhaustive discussion of significant observations, but rather it represents some of the more salient issues that cut across many of the concerns we have identified with regard to the group of collective bargaining agreements and labor management relations as a whole.[2]

The foregoing conclusions about the union contracts in the Toledo school district underscore an important consideration. The Toledo peer review program was established and is maintained in an extremely pro-union environment. Beyond a reasonable doubt, the Toledo district has tolerated a substantial number of highly inefficient personnel policies and practices; praise for its peer review program must be assessed in this context. As the items from the Long/Clark report on the TFT contract illustrate, the Toledo peer review program exists in a district that has subordinated student achievement and taxpayer interests to union interests to an unprecedented extent. It does not necessarily follow that the Toledo peer review program is undesirable, but the contractual environment justifies a cautious attitude toward district support for peer review programs. The same point applies to at least some of the other highly publicized peer review districts, especially Columbus and Rochester. Like the Toledo contract, the Columbus contract is a long, detailed document that restricts managerial discretion in a myriad of ways; even when the district retains discretion, the requirement that it consult with the union before acting is bound to result in co-management by the CEA.

   A three-year contract reached in Columbus in October 1997 continued the pattern of generous settlements in the past. For example, although Columbus schools are open for only 180 days, the teachers are paid for 196 days, including holidays, professional meetings, parent conferences, and record-keeping. Nevertheless, Columbus teachers are eligible for fifteen days of sick leave annually, available for either the teacher or the illness of a member of the teacher's family. Although the district had estimated that Columbus teachers used an average of nine days of sick leave a year (one for every twenty days school was in session), the contractual resolution was to require a doctor's certificate after a teacher missed ten days in the school year, or after any time a teacher missed two or more days in a row. In addition, the payments for unused sick leave were increased so that a teacher with an M.A. degree plus thirty credits and twenty-seven years experience, who retired with 406 days of unused sick leave, would be entitled to approximately $40,000 for accumulated sick leave.

By 1997, CEA president John Grossman had outlasted nine Columbus superintendents; it is hardly surprising that he is widely regarded as the most powerful leader in the district. In Rochester, the site of another highly publicized peer review program, community disenchantment with extremely generous union contracts led to sweeping changes in school board membership and in the superintendency.[3] Such facts suggest that union power, not the merits of peer review, is the main factor in its emergence.

Peer review should not be rejected because it is a union initiative and is operative only in districts characterized by an extremely strong union presence. Nonetheless, the record to date indicates that peer review has yet to take hold in other districts. This fact suggests that peer review's appeal to teachers and teacher unions does not and will not necessarily translate into an attractive initiative for school boards.

If peer review is desirable on the basis of its educational merits, we should expect that school districts would accept it even in the absence of pressure from teacher unions. Clearly, however, the "model" peer review plans are in districts with extremely powerful teacher unions. Media and professional treatment of peer review has overlooked this point, but the contracts in peer review districts confirm the fact that peer review plans are associated with highly expensive concessions to teachers and severe limitations on school management. Anyone who doubts this should review copies of the contracts in the leading peer review districts.

9

Peer Review: Summary and Conclusions

In 1997, in its submission to the fact finder in its contract dispute with the Toledo school district, the Toledo Federation of Teachers (TFT) asserted:

> Toledo's peer review system has been the model and standard for evaluation reform efforts not only in Ohio, but throughout the nation. Within the past month, North Carolina, with Governor Hunt in the lead, California, and Florida have asked Toledo for help in setting up peer evaluation systems. About 6,000 calls and letters have been received over the life of the Toledo Plan. All major television networks have featured Toledo as has PBS. The leading newspapers and magazines have written about what we do. The NEA, long an opponent of peer review, recently changed its policy and Toledo people worked behind the scenes to advise NEA officials about the processes necessary to adopt peer review.
>
> Cincinnati, Columbus, and several smaller districts in Ohio have adopted the Toledo model. Governor Voinovich has been instrumental in getting the Ohio Department of Education to adopt peer review in the state's new teacher licensure system that is now coming on line. The governor is a strong supporter of the Toledo Plan. Toledo people have been involved in that process, and we were recently awarded a large grant from the Ohio Department of Education to develop an implementation procedure for other Ohio districts. This superintendent [i.e., Merrill Grant, superintendent of the Toledo public schools] refused to sign the grant application for two months. The University of Toledo was a co-recipient of the grant and finally persuaded the superintendent to sign. The deputy superintendent of the Ohio Department of Education also made calls.[1]

The TFT submission raises an interesting issue. What weight should be given to the widespread favorable publicity about peer review? A few examples may help to answer this question.

Perhaps the earliest national recognition of the Toledo program was a 1984 Rand study that did not discuss most of the issues raised here. The study did discuss the costs of the program very briefly but grossly underestimated the actual costs.[2]

More recently, a 1996 book entitled *United Mind Workers* illustrates the pattern of peer review analysis. Like other praise for peer review, the book ignores its costs. Referring to peer review in Toledo, the authors state:

> But the important matter is that in ten years, thirty-five poor teachers have either left the district or improved as a result of the cooperative work between the district and the union. Most important, this represents a major change from the traditional protective stance of unions to a position in which the union works with administration to improve or remove the least effective members of the teaching force.[3]

The year after these comments were made, the Toledo public school system bargained to impasse with the Toledo Federation of Teachers over district efforts to evaluate the 41 percent of the teaching staff who are not evaluated at all under the peer review plan. It is unlikely that an objective study of peer review in Toledo would have ignored administration criticisms of the plan, or would have failed to mention them. The fact that the TFT threatened to strike over the district's proposed changes in the peer review program hardly suggests a change from "the traditional protective stance of unions."

The National Commission on Teaching and America's Future is the source of another recent prestigious endorsement of peer review. The commission, however, included the NEA and AFT presidents, leaders of organizations directly dependent on NEA/AFT support of one kind or another, and politicians who have received substantial union support during their political careers. Not surprisingly, the commission endorsed peer review, but there is no evidence in the report itself, or in the list of the commission's members, consultants, and advisors, that the commission considered the views of any critic of peer review. For that matter, it is doubtful whether the commission considered the views of union critics on any issue; the commission concluded:

> Teacher organizations for the 21st century have improved student learning at the heart of their mission. Through their collective voice, teacher unions have argued for better preparation, the hiring of qualified teachers, and better conditions in schools because they know that gains on these fronts are gains for students. They

have begun to push for greater professionalism and to challenge the status quo within their own ranks. Although there is a need to build more secure bridges between unions and school boards, recent efforts point the way to a new era in which teacher organizations and local policymakers join forces on behalf of student advocacy and professional accountability.[4]

This is not the place to debate the commission's benign view of teacher unions; but obviously its praise for peer review emanates from an extremely pro-union source, if not from the unions themselves.

One additional incident is highly revealing. In mid-December 1997, I learned about a $116,000 grant from the Ohio Department of Education to the University of Toledo for a peer review project. Thereupon, I called the professor administering the grant to find out the purpose of it. The purpose turned out to be preparation and dissemination of a packet of materials to assist Ohio school districts in initiating peer review plans. In response to my inquiry, the project director conceded that the packet included no discussion or analysis of the costs of peer review.

Granted, I have not scrutinized every publication praising peer review, but as the examples suggest, peer review cannot be justified merely on the basis of its testimonials or favorable national publicity. To be meaningful, favorable reports about peer review must rely on more than favorable union versions of it. Inasmuch as the favorable reports fail to raise the issues considered in this study, the reports are not a persuasive argument for peer review.

A Time Perspective on Peer Review

In K–12 education, peer review is a recent development. Although mentioned from time to time in the 1980s, peer review was not widely regarded as a major reform initiative until the mid-1990s, when NEA President Bob Chase treated it as the major initiative of his term of office as president.

How long will it take for peer review to become widely adopted? The answer to this question is hardly encouraging to anyone who regards peer review as a major reform. In the AFT, peer review was introduced in Toledo in 1981. Columbus adopted its peer review program in 1986. Despite widespread national publicity, especially about these two plans, AFT locals have shown little or no interest in pursuing the matter. Management opposition has not been a factor; what management's attitude would be if AFT locals were aggressively negotiating over peer review remains to be seen, but it would probably be negative for the reasons mentioned previously.

Although much larger, the NEA has very few peer review districts. In fact, Columbus is the only large NEA affiliate that utilizes peer review as a termination procedure as well as for assistance. Until its 1997 convention, NEA policy discouraged peer review. Resolution New D-6, adopted at the NEA's 1997 convention, removed the discouragement but did not embrace the concept. This resolution merely states that some locals will find peer review to be a useful idea, and it then spells out a laundry list of conditions that should be observed in implementing peer review plans. Although state and local affiliates are the ones who will have to adopt peer review, the NEA/AFT leadership is aggressively promoting it. These union leaders may not enjoy much success along this line; in a recent NEA online poll, 72 percent of the respondents opposed having NEA affiliates help get rid of bad teachers; only 28 percent supported the idea.[5]

We cannot expect local school boards and school administrators to rush forward with peer review proposals; peer review requires an initiative by a local union. It is difficult, however, to see how or why peer review should be a high union priority in most school districts. For better or for worse, huge growth in peer review plans is doubtful, even with strong NEA support and encouragement for locals interested in trying it. To be sure, since NEA president Bob Chase endorsed peer review in 1996, the Columbus Education Association has reportedly received over twelve hundred inquiries about its peer review program, but this surge of interest has yet to result in many adoptions of peer review.

Most teacher union contracts are multi-year and will not expire in any one year. Many of the expiring contracts will be in districts that are too small to embrace peer review effectively. In many others, it is unlikely that local affiliates can be persuaded to accord peer review a high priority; indeed, as the debate at the 1997 NEA convention demonstrated, many locals oppose peer review in principle. In districts where the local is willing to negotiate peer review, school management may be opposed. In the small number of districts that agree to adopt a peer review program, it will take at least a year to establish it, provide the training, and orient various parties to their roles and responsibilities under peer review. Finally, note that peer review is likely to apply only to new teachers, especially in the first few years of implementation. Assuming 10 percent turnover, it is very doubtful that even 1 percent of the nation's teachers will have been subject to peer review by the year 2000. The overwhelming majority of new teachers would be employed by school districts in the absence of any kind of peer review program.

There appears to be no research on the career pattern of interns who are not rehired in peer review districts. Consequently, peer review may affect *where* these interns teach much more than whether they teach at all. In some states, such as Michigan, the unions have negotiated "mentor teacher" clauses that pay tenured teachers a bonus for helping new teachers. These clauses do not require the mentors to make recommendations on the employment status of new teachers; they are the "assistance only" version of peer review and are subject to the comments previously made about that version of it. It is doubtful whether the unions in mentor districts will opt for peer review as an evaluation procedure inasmuch as their teachers are being paid as mentors while avoiding the problems inherent in supervisory versions of peer review.

The Toledo experience suggests that it will take a very long time for peer review to become widely adopted in American education. Toledo employs about 175 new teachers annually, out of a total of about 2,500. Under both the conventional system and peer review, the overwhelming majority of new teachers have their contracts renewed. To justify peer review, it would be necessary to show significant differences in the renewal rate and/or differences with respect to which teachers are renewed and which are terminated. How big must a difference be to be "significant"? Opinions will differ, but I am not aware of any peer review program that has addressed the issue.

The new teachers in Toledo comprise about 7 percent of the district's total teaching force. Assume that renewals under peer review differ from conventional review processes by 10 percent of the new hires. On an annual basis, peer review in Toledo would result in less than 1 percent difference in the district's teaching force. Obviously, the district staff would be overwhelmingly the same regardless of the presence or absence of peer review. Despite all the union promotion of peer review, it has very little potential for improving education.

The data on terminations of tenured teachers also indicates that any improvements due to peer review will be minuscule. As we have seen, over a twelve-year period, only forty-four teachers in Toledo, out of a 2,500-member teaching force, were subjected to intervention by a peer review team. Of these, twelve were restored to their teaching position without restriction; most of the remaining thirty-two retired, resigned, or were terminated. There is no data on what would have happened in the absence of peer review. In view of the fact that the district probably employed about 4,000 tenured teachers during this period, the peer review program clearly played a minor role even in this showcase district.

Despite the tremendous amount of publicity it has received, peer review will probably affect only an extremely small number of teachers for many years to come. The reason is that not many districts are likely to adopt peer review. Clearly, even on its own assumptions, peer review is not feasible in small school districts. Consider a district that employs 150 teachers, and hires about fifteen new teachers a year, distributed over the various grades from kindergarten through the twelfth grade. It would be highly uneconomical to pay teachers a

$5,000–$5,900 stipend for three years to supervise a handful of teachers, especially since the new teachers, at least at the secondary levels, will ordinarily be teaching different subjects. It would be difficult to specify the number of teachers required to implement peer review effectively, but it will clearly exclude the majority of districts, albeit not necessarily the districts that enroll the most pupils in toto.[6]

Some supporters of peer review believe that cooperative arrangements among small school districts will enable them to participate in peer review plans. Although this option cannot be excluded as a possibility, and not withstanding the fact that the Ohio Department of Education has allocated funds for this purpose, the additional coordination problems suggest that the possibility will not materialize very often. In small districts, parents and administrators have a good idea of how teachers are performing; the information is virtually unavoidable. The parents and administrators see all the teachers frequently at the schools and often at community functions as well; there is seldom any thought that formal evaluation is necessary, although it may be required by statute or union contract.

As of the fall of 1997, it appeared that at least four NEA state affiliates (California, New Jersey, West Virginia, and Wisconsin), comprising 21 percent of NEA membership, had taken some action that reflected opposition to peer review. Elsewhere, the union contracts will not expire for one to three years. Many local associations are opposed to peer review; that much is evident from the 1997 NEA convention and from the slow, indeed, hardly perceptible, rate of its implementation by AFT locals. In Toledo, it took the TFT nine years to achieve school board acceptance of a peer review plan aggressively promoted by a TFT president who was thoroughly secure in his leadership position. Granted, the TFT did not have other alleged success stories to cite, but it will be astonishing if school boards accept peer review the first time it is laid on the table. Inasmuch as the NEA recommends against peer review programs that do not include certain contractual safeguards for consulting teachers, peer review may never get off the ground in the thirteen states that have not enacted teacher bargaining statutes. The foregoing list of obstacles is not exhaustive, but it should suffice to show that peer review will not be widely adopted for many years to come.

The Effectiveness of Peer Review

Theoretically, the ultimate criterion for evaluating peer review should be its effects on student achievement related to its costs. This criterion is extremely difficult to apply; hence, it is understandable why the effectiveness of peer review is discussed largely in terms of its impact on teachers. If peer review minimizes the number of poor teachers, it is assumed that the outcome will be increased student achievement.

Although this common-sense assumption is reasonable, the TFT also relies upon test scores to support its arguments for peer review. For example, in defending its position to the fact finder in the 1997 negotiations, the TFT cited a state report showing that a higher percentage of Toledo's ninth graders passed proficiency tests in writing, reading, and citizenship than ninth graders in Cincinnati, Cleveland, Columbus, Akron, and Dayton, the other five of Ohio's six largest school districts. In addition, the Toledo ninth graders ranked second highest in mathematics proficiency.

These data do not constitute a serious argument for peer review. In 1995, after fourteen years of peer review, Toledo ninth graders had virtually the lowest scores among the six largest Ohio districts. Consequently, the high 1997 ranking cannot be attributed to peer review. Indeed, in a *Toledo Blade* article on the test scores, "Toledo school officials attribute[d] the improvement in part to a concerted effort that involved tutoring, calling parents, in-school conferences, and summer classes." Peer review was not cited as a factor, one way or the other.[7]

Presumably, the effectiveness of peer review will affect the rate at which it is adopted by school districts. On this assumption, there is little or no reason to anticipate rapid, widespread adoption of peer review.

In Toledo, most of the regular teachers have come through the peer review process. At no time, however, has anyone, including peer review's strongest supporters, demonstrated that pupil achievement has gone up as a result of peer review. The claim has been that peer review results in better support for new teachers and a more effective procedure for terminating incompetent tenured teachers; presumably, pupil achievement will improve as a result. Nevertheless, no one has demonstrated the relationship between these allegedly better personnel practices, and pupil achievement. The relationship is merely assumed, without any evidence whatsoever of its magnitude. And if this is true for the model peer review district, we can hardly expect better results in districts that are just beginning to adopt peer review plans.

One's reaction may be that pupil achievement is affected by several factors, and that it is unrealistic to expect peer review to overcome the effects of single-parenthood, drug abuse, delinquency, and other negative influences affecting educational achievement. The response must be that the supporters of peer review cannot have it both ways. If peer review cannot demonstrate a beneficial impact on pupil achievement after it has been in effect for seventeen years, why all the attention paid to it as the new union priority? Intellectual integrity requires that if a beneficial impact on pupil achievement cannot be demonstrated, the claims made for peer review be adjusted downward; the union-sponsored "reform" turns out to be just as unproved as any other.

In fact, candor requires recognition of the possibility that peer review may result in a lower quality of instruction. We cannot assert this outcome to be the case, but it is more than a remote possibility. Every year, a school district implementing peer review takes a number of excellent teachers out of the classroom. If it were not for peer review, these consulting teachers would remain in their classrooms and the district would require fewer interns. For example, suppose the district has 171 vacancies. Under peer review, the district must employ 190 new teachers because interns must be employed to fill the positions of the nineteen consulting teachers employed to supervise 171 interns.

What is the evidence that the nineteen consulting teachers bring about sufficient improvement among the students of the 190 interns to justify the salaries and expenses of the consulting teachers? Not even the most ardent supporters of peer review have been able to cite any improvement in student achievement clearly attributable to peer review that justifies the expenditures.

A School Board Perspective on Peer Review

Like any personnel process, peer review is subject to error. Our choice is not between a process subject to error and one that is free from error. It is how best to maximize sound personnel decisions at a reasonable cost. The cost factor should not be overlooked. It is almost always possible to improve the quality of personnel decisions, but we are not likely to do so if the costs are prohibitive. As I have noted, for example, a school district personnel director might check out ten references instead of three, but the improvement in hiring decisions might not be worth the additional costs. Analogously, peer review might have some beneficial effects, but the benefits may not be worth the additional costs.

Another problem is that the outcomes of peer review are interpreted in a way that reflects credit on the program even when the results are contradictory. For example, in Columbus, the union president has asserted that "[t]he most important issue for us is that we have helped increase the number of beginning teachers who are staying in the profession. Experts have told us that only 50 percent of beginning teachers in urban districts are around after three years."[8]

This is a very ambiguous standard of success. First, the criterion assumes that there is a high level of talent among teachers hired in Columbus, as well as in teacher education programs. Second, when standards are the issue, most observers point to a higher, not a lower, failure rate as evidence of higher standards. A company that hires everyone who applies would not normally be regarded as having higher standards than a company that terminates a higher proportion of new employees. The most critical point, however, is that the higher retention rate of new teachers might be due to several factors unrelated to teaching competence; for example, a school district might retain more teachers because it lacks the funds to recruit better ones.

One of the most troublesome facts about the claims made for peer review is that they appear to be contradictory. In Columbus, peer review is deemed a success because the district retains a higher percentage of new teachers, whereas in Toledo, peer review is deemed a success because it lowered the same percentage. The argument is that in Toledo before the introduction of peer review, virtually all of the new teachers were rehired. This supposedly illustrates the lack of standards prior to peer review. But if the retention rate for new teachers is the test of success, and peer review is a success whether the retention rate goes up or down, "success" is meaningless.

The absence of reliable data on outcomes as well as costs suggests a cautious if not skeptical approach to the desirability of peer review. Nevertheless, in the next few years, we can expect a surge in union proposals on peer review.[9] Inasmuch as union contracts vary in duration, most school boards will not be asked to accept peer review immediately; however, a considerable number will be faced with proposals on the subject as they negotiate successor contracts. How should they respond?

First, they should treat union proposals on peer review as they would proposals on any topic. This means that the district negotiators should require the union to respond to the issues raised in this analysis. A list of such issues should include the following:

- What are the objectives of peer review?
- What are the criteria to measure progress toward the objectives?
- What will be the total costs of the program?
- How long will it take to decide whether peer review is a cost-effective way of improving instruction?
- Is a proposal to have members of the bargaining unit observe and/or evaluate other members within the scope of negotiations?
- Will consulting teachers be evaluated on how effectively they serve in this capacity? If they will be, how and by whom will such evaluation be carried out? And if the consulting teachers are not to be evaluated for service in this capacity, doesn't the proposal for peer review avoid individual accountability for a very important personnel function?
- To whom will teachers appeal if they wish to challenge the recommendations of peer reviewers?
- What provisions are or would be in place to protect the rights of nonunion or antiunion teachers, or teachers critical of incumbent union leadership?
- How are consulting teachers to be appointed?
- How will challenges to union officers who are consulting teachers receive a fair hearing?

- Does peer review replace the tenure hearings provided by the state tenure law? If not, isn't the process merely another hurdle that the district must overcome to dismiss incompetent teachers?
- Will teachers who are not rehired as a result of peer review be eligible to teach elsewhere? If so, how can peer review be considered a step toward professional status?
- Are there any costs of peer review to the union? To the peer reviewers?

Unless and until the district receives satisfactory answers to such questions, it should not accept proposals to initiate peer review. In raising the questions, district negotiators should make it clear that raising them does not imply tacit acceptance of the proposal in some form. I deem it unlikely that any union can provide adequate answers to the questions listed, but adequacy is in the eye of the beholder. Generally speaking, it would also be inadvisable to agree to a joint committee to study proposals for peer review. Such joint committees usually prolong bargaining. Peer review is a union proposal; unless and until the union can make a persuasive case for it in some form, the district should not accept it. Instead, the district negotiators should counter with proposals that enable school management to dismiss incompetent teachers without the all-out opposition of the union.

One salutary effect of proposals for peer review should be a critical review of district evaluation procedures and results. How many teachers have received negative evaluations? Are there significant differences in the frequency of negative evaluations by principals in different schools? If so, what is the reason? Do employment practices keep employment of poor prospects to a minimum? School districts should raise these questions even in the absence of proposals for peer review.

Instead of turning to peer review, school boards might insist upon an analysis of teacher evaluations. Many would be shocked to discover how few negative evaluations occur in their schools. The solution to poor screening of new teachers, or inadequate supervision of tenured teachers, may not be a complex and convoluted plan for peer review. It may require only the replacement of various administrative personnel who are not performing adequately.

As I noted in Chapter 6, supporters of peer review claim the following benefits from it:

- More accurate identification of teachers who should not remain in the profession.
- Career-saving assistance to new teachers who would leave teaching if it were not for the help they received from the peer review program.
- A more collaborative spirit between the union and the administration.
- Higher teacher morale as a result of the stipends for consulting teachers and the utilization of teacher expertise.

- More time for principals to perform the tasks that they are better equipped and situated to perform.
- A decrease in litigation, or in the threat of litigation, over termination of teachers.

As a practical matter, it is virtually impossible to quantify most of these benefits. Even when the benefits are quantifiable, the proponents of peer review have not quantified them; for example, CEA president John Grossman pointed out that peer review has reduced litigation over tenure in Columbus, but provided no data on the issue. Even assuming that these benefits exist, cost/benefit analysis of peer review is virtually nonexistent. As a result, interests play a major role in the acceptance or rejection of peer review. These interests include the greatly enhanced power of the teacher union, and the teacher interest in receiving a substantial stipend for a few years. Although some of the benefits are plausible, they lack the research support that is required for their acceptance. Furthermore, the pervasive neglect of the costs of peer review undermines most of the claims made for it.

As far as new teachers are concerned, the outcomes under peer review probably do not differ materially from the outcomes under conventional evaluation procedures. If there are any significant differences, they are probably due to the fact that school administrators believe that their recommendations to fire teachers are more likely to be sustained if the teacher union supports, or at least does not contest, the decision, and to the fact that much more time is available under peer review for assisting, observing, and evaluating new teachers. In Columbus, the consulting teachers observe the interns at least twenty times for a total of at least fifty hours. In addition, the consulting teachers must confer with each intern for at least fifty hours during the year, and it is deemed highly desirable that a consulting teacher spend at least one full day with each of his or her interns. Obviously, this is much more time than principals devote to these tasks; again, the issue is whether the additional benefits that may result are worth the additional cost. To say the least, the evidence to this effect is not very persuasive, especially since the cost factors are invariably ignored in favorable evaluations of peer review. In any event, there is no credible evidence that peer review leads to significantly different judgments about teacher competence, when compared to conventional methods of administrative evaluation.

Peer review districts sometimes maintain data on various aspects of their programs. For example, the districts (or the participating unions) sometimes maintain databases that compare teacher attrition before and after initiation of peer review. Although useful for certain purposes, such data cannot establish the value of peer review. To see why, suppose that the district retains a higher proportion of new teachers under peer review than under conventional procedures. By itself, this fact proves nothing; it is consistent with unfavorable as well as favorable evaluations of peer review. The teacher unions can point to the fact as evidence that peer review helps teachers become qualified for employment; critics can point to the same fact as evidence that school districts lower their standards for employment as a result of peer review. The proponents of peer review have simply assumed that the decisions made pursuant to the process are good decisions; the administrative outcomes, such as the attrition rates, are then interpreted to validate the assumption. In the meantime, we have no information, or way to get it, that demonstrates a beneficial classroom impact of peer review. Such an impact is assumed, not demonstrated, in the research data on peer review.

Aside from the fact that most school districts do not maintain useful databases on evaluation and attrition issues, the evidence supporting peer review rests upon an assumption that seems highly doubtful. The literature on peer review invariably assumes that the talent level of new teachers remains the same from year to year. The fact is, however, that major demographic and economic changes have characterized the leading peer review districts. It is not likely that the talent level among new teachers has remained constant over long periods of time. I do not know how the changes in the talent level of teachers would affect the claims made for peer review; my point is that the absence of any attention to the issue suggests a weak evidentiary standard for peer review's efficacy.

In view of the lack of data on peer review, and the absence of independent evaluation of its costs and benefits, it seems remarkable that the teacher unions, especially the NEA, should promote it so aggressively. As I have noted, when the NEA opposes a reform, it insists upon long trial periods, data on every conceivable aspect, and irrefutable evidence of benefits. Otherwise, all such reforms are labeled "fads," "quick fixes," or with some other pejorative that implies lack of substance. Obviously, the standards of proof for reforms opposed by the unions are higher (often to the point of practical impossibility) than the standards for reforms they support. As structured and implemented in a few school districts, peer review provides substantial financial benefits for teachers and a huge public-relations coup for the unions. With virtually no critical analysis, the media are already praising the unions for helping to terminate incompetent teachers. Instead of analyzing the specifics, the media treat peer review as a watershed development, a break from traditional unionism.[10] Little or no mention is made of the fact that a substantial number of teachers are paid more to do less, that peer review increases a union's power over its members, that tenured teachers avoid evaluation altogether, and that peer review involves substantial costs, to mention a few of the more salient omissions. Peer review illustrates the point that, for certain purposes, the belief that educational reform is taking place is more important than the reality. The teacher unions depend on the perception to maintain the status quo. Peer review may add a year or two to the perception, but its major practical effect will be to extend teacher union control over public education.

This negative assessment of peer review raises an obvious question: What can and should the teacher unions do to raise the level of teacher performance? In answering this question, I assume that the structure of public education and the union role continue as they are. In other words, the following suggestions do not assume any drastic changes in our educational system; they can be implemented within the existing structure of public education, and their acceptance would strengthen both public education and respect for teacher unions. This is not to say that more basic changes are not necessary or desirable; in my opinion, they are, and they would be even if the teacher unions implemented the suggestions that follow. Nevertheless, remedying the problems of teacher tenure and of terminating incompetent teachers does not necessarily require a drastically different system of education.

Preliminarily, it is doubtful whether teacher tenure, whether by statute or union contract, is the most important negative influence of teacher unionization. Teacher tenure has been carried to excessive lengths, and it is a topic that calls for reexamination of the union's role; but in terms of its impact on educational achievement, it is not the issue that should receive the highest priority. Nevertheless, because of its prominence in the new unionism, we should consider what the new unionism might do without threatening the basic structure of the old unionism.

First, the unions should accept a prompt and fair procedure for resolving tenure cases. The existing arrangements are as indefensible as the complete absence of protections was in an earlier day. For example, consider a teacher who alleges ethnic or religious discrimination in a tenure decision. The teacher may be protected by a tenure law and a collective bargaining contract. In addition, there may be local, state, and federal statutes prohibiting such discrimination. Thus, we have gone from the absence of legal protection to a situation in which teachers can choose among a host of legal protections. Both of these extremes are undesirable.

There are several ways the unions could minimize excessive tenure protections without eliminating tenure entirely. For example, they could agree that all grievances, including claims of discriminatory treatment, would be resolved only through the grievance procedure. The unions could agree not to support claims that could be raised in other forums; alternatively, they could insist that the filing of a grievance constituted a waiver of any other remedy on the substance of the grievance. This solution does not waive anyone's statutory rights because the grievant could, at his or her sole discretion, choose to exercise these rights rather than filing a contractual grievance. Furthermore, this solution is consistent with the rationale for collective bargaining, namely, that employment relations should be resolved insofar as possible in the workplace by the parties involved. The unions should also agree to a grievance procedure that provides expeditious and final resolution of claims related to dismissals.

In many if not most districts, the teacher unions could negotiate such arrangements without any special justification for doing so. If such justification were needed, the arrangements could be a quid pro quo for a salary raise or insurance benefits. Actually, school boards can and have sometimes negotiated such arrangements, and many more could do so if they made the effort.

If employment relations are to be settled by collective bargaining between teacher unions and school boards, the state legislatures should get out of the business of legislating terms and conditions of teacher employment. Conceptually, therefore, the states that enacted teacher bargaining statutes should have simultaneously repealed the teacher tenure statutes. For various reasons, this did not happen; the states that enacted bargaining laws have also expanded the statutory benefits and protections for teachers. Inasmuch as the teacher unions cannot allow the repeal of the tenure statutes for political reasons, what can they do to move away from their excessive protection of teachers charged with incompetence?

One possibility is for the union and school management to agree to arbitrate statutory tenure claims with tight time limits. That is, instead of relying on cumbersome legal processes, during which teachers are paid while waiting for their cases to be tried, the unions could agree to have arbitrators resolve the issues. Such an agreement would have many benefits for the unions, and school management should be careful in making or responding to such proposals. Nevertheless, if a reasonable accommodation on the issue is the objective, this solution should be considered. It reveals that there are solutions to tenure disputes that do not require the union to usurp management's role in personnel matters.

Another constructive action that teacher unions could take relates to course work taken by teachers for salary credit. The conventional union position is that teachers know best what courses they need to improve their classroom performance. Consequently, the unions bargain for proposals that allow salary credit for any courses taken by teachers. The upshot is that teachers get salary credit for courses that are the easiest, the most convenient, or the least expensive, or courses that are needed to become an administrator or enter a different profession, or to facilitate a teacher's business, or those that are available by correspondence—the list of indefensible reasons why many teachers take many courses is endless. Needless to say, school management deserves strong criticism for this state of affairs—more so than the teacher unions, which are acting as their members want them to act. Nevertheless, union leaders who are serious about having the unions play a more constructive role can usually effectuate significant improvement on this widely neglected issue.

To reiterate, these are actions most union leaders can take without risk to their leadership positions. And if they cannot, their inability to do so undermines the basic case for collective bargaining in public education. It would be tantamount to conceding that teachers collectively will not accept reasonable restrictions on union power to block management, or on teachers' freedom to pursue their self-interest at the expense of the public interest. Union negotiators often concede (privately) that management proposals are reasonable and desirable, but also plead inability to persuade union members to accept the proposals. Every such case—and there are huge numbers of them—is evidence that teachers and teacher unions will not be the vanguard of educational reform.

10

Beyond Peer Review:
The New Unionism That Is Needed

The fact that the status quo is not acceptable does not justify every alternative to it; however, if the NEA/AFT version of the "new unionism" is not acceptable, what kind of new unionism would be?

It would not be helpful to outline an ideal new unionism that has no chance whatsoever of becoming a reality, even as a goal. Whatever one thinks about the teacher unions as they are, various individuals and groups benefit from the status quo. These beneficiaries are not simply union officers and staff. They include arbitrators, mediators, and labor lawyers who depend on the existing structure of labor/management relations for their livelihood. The opponents of change also include academics who would have to change their courses and research and, most painful of all, their way of thinking about unions. Fundamental change almost invariably threatens some parties with a stake in the status quo, and these parties will resist change in a variety of ways.

In this context, the prospects for basic change in the teacher unions are not very promising. The NEA and the AFT employ over six thousand full-time employees in toto. Over half earn more than $100,000 a year in salary and benefits, and not many could earn as much in any other occupation; hence, we must anticipate intense union opposition toward any threat to the status quo in union employment.[1] Despite all the publicity about the new unionism, there has been no significant change in NEA/AFT budgets or personnel. Facts such as these suggest that one should take a cautious attitude toward claims that the new unionism reflects a basic change in NEA/AFT programs or policies.

The foregoing considerations do not imply that the quest for a new unionism is hopeless. They suggest, however, that only an external threat is likely to generate basic changes in the teacher unions. The most obvious threats are privatization in one form or another: vouchers, tuition tax credits, contracting out, and home schooling are threats to the public school monopoly, and hence to NEA/AFT power. Needless to say, the NEA and the AFT oppose all such efforts; in fact, opposition to privatization is their top priority. Absent a credible threat to the status quo, the most that we can expect is a few union concessions on the most egregious abuses of union power.

Nevertheless, the new unionism should not be viewed as a struggle between the supporters of public education and the supporters of privatization. On the contrary, the critical strategic issues involve the supporters of public education who are deeply concerned about the excessive power of the teacher unions. Different parties can agree on a course of action without necessarily having the same motives or reasons for doing so; if public school supporters concerned about excessive teacher union power team up with the privatizers to curb that power, the NEA and the AFT could be forced to accept basic changes within a relatively short period of time. The question is: What changes are desirable from a public policy standpoint? The following suggestions are not exhaustive, but they would go a long way toward remedying the deficiencies in the existing unions. To reiterate, the issue is not whether the NEA and the AFT will initiate the changes; it is whether pressure can be brought to bear to force their acceptance of them.

The Critical Importance of Options

It is absolutely critical to recognize that more options are needed. Specifically, there should be options with respect to the system of representation as well as options relating to choice of representative; it is essential to avoid the mind-set that assumes that the choices are limited to unfettered managerial discretion on the one hand, or collective bargaining as we know it on the other. It may not be essential to repeal the state bargaining laws, but it is essential to allow teachers to choose a less adversarial system and/or representative organization. In any case, we should be careful not to replace one straitjacket with a different one.

Granted, the NEA, the AFT, and other public-sector unions will adamantly oppose any suggestion that would provide real options to their entrenched positions; their tremendous resources will render it extremely difficult to establish either competing systems of representation or competing organizations.

Nevertheless, unless and until an effort is made, negative conclusions about the prospects for success may be premature.[2]

Alternative systems of representation should be especially welcome in small school districts, which I shall arbitrarily define as districts that employ less than a hundred full-time teachers. National labor policy was established to solve various problems in large industrial plants such as auto manufacturers. When the states enacted bargaining laws for public employees in the 1960s and 1970s, they tended to copy the framework incorporated in federal law, which always excluded small establishments. Naturally, the unions that drafted and lobbied for the state bargaining statutes omitted any exclusion of small government units, such as small school districts.

In practice, however, collective bargaining tends to erode staff collegiality in small school districts. Teachers, administrators, and parents in such districts tend to know each other at a personal as well as a professional level. Because of the small scale, the teachers must usually perform a wider variety of duties; this tendency conflicts with collective bargaining, which emphasizes minimizing the differences among teachers in compensation, load, and assignment. Furthermore, small districts are much less likely to experience the problems that require bargaining time or expertise; for example, transfers are not a problem if there is only one site. Seniority is seldom an issue when teachers are responsible for different subjects and grade levels. When several teachers want to be the next department chairperson, it may be desirable to negotiate a procedure to resolve the issue, but no such procedure is necessary if there is no department. One can argue that differences in district size will be reflected in the bargaining process itself, but the stronger argument is that differences in size justify differences in the system of representation.

Minority Representation

One of the valid criticisms of exclusive representation is its inherent tendency to result in inequitable treatment for occupational minorities. Whenever a small number of highly paid occupations are represented by a union that is composed largely of workers in lesser paid occupations, the former are consistently disadvantaged in collective bargaining. The reason is that the unions respond to what most of their members want, and most do not want large differentials between their pay and the pay of their fellow workers.

Representation of occupational minorities is a pervasive problem in education. The fate of mathematics teachers under collective bargaining illustrates the problem. The noneducational demand for the kind of talent required to be a good mathematics teacher is much greater than for the talent required to be a good elementary teacher. If teacher employment were more oriented to market forces, mathematics teachers would be paid more than elementary teachers. As matters stand, persons with mathematical talents tend not to become mathematics teachers because all teachers are paid the same regardless of grade level or subject. Of course, some mathematics teachers in the public schools are mathematically talented, but the proportion is much lower than it would be if teacher unions allowed salary differentials based on the market demand for different kinds of talent. The unions cannot or at least will not allow this under exclusive representation because doing so would lead to division within the union. Subgroups within the union would be fighting over the differentials instead of focusing all of their efforts on obtaining more benefits for everyone from the school boards.

In short, union dynamics are responsible not only for the inequitable treatment of occupational minorities, but for salary policies that weaken American education everywhere. The need to avoid division within the unions is the reason that the teacher unions promote the fiction that the major incentive to go into teaching is an interest in helping young people. The reality is that, talentwise, teachers are more like other workers who deal with the same subject matter than they are like other teachers; for example, art teachers are more like other workers in the arts than they are like other teachers. Inasmuch as candid recognition of this fact would undermine single salary schedules and hence unity within the unions, the unions promote the idea that love of children is the reason why persons enter teaching.

Theoretically, or perhaps "technically" would be a more accurate term, this problem can be remedied within the present framework of teacher representation. Teachers in various fields can submit petitions to be severed from the bargaining unit in order to be represented by a union of their own choosing. Although this is theoretically possible, the legal and practical obstacles to such a solution are virtually impossible to overcome under the present framework. What is essential is a framework in which a minority of teachers, perhaps only 5 or 10 percent, can achieve representation of their own choosing merely upon showing a requisite number of teachers who support the request. Minimally, such a change would exert strong pressures on the teacher unions to recognize and deal with the legitimate demands of subgroups that are always outvoted within the union.

Multiple Systems of Employee Benefits

At the present time, teachers enjoy a dual system of benefits: statutory and contractual. For example, most states have tenure laws that protect teachers against unjust dismissals. Notwithstanding, the unions continue to bargain for contractual protection, usually in the form of a provision requiring that disciplinary action must be for "just cause." In addition, teachers, like other public employees, enjoy statutory and/or constitutional protection against dismissals (actually, protection against adverse action generally) on the basis of race, gender, disability, age, and political orientation.

At the present time, the teacher who alleges racial discrimination to be the reason for his or her dismissal has multiple remedies, and the choice of one does not necessarily result in denial of other forums in which to press the teacher's claim. The union and the teacher simply survey the remedies and select the forum that offers the best chance for success.

This situation is contrary to the rationale for teacher bargaining as it was articulated during the 1960s and 1970s, when state legislatures adopted the teacher bargaining statutes. The rationale then was that employment relations in public education should be resolved by good-faith bargaining between school boards and teacher unions. Statutory protections were deemed to be too slow, too cumbersome, too expensive, and too rigid to resolve the varied problems that arise.

An actual case illustrates the problem. California law provides that teachers convicted of felonies shall be dismissed. Pursuant to this statutory mandate, a school district fired a teacher convicted of cultivating marijuana on the teacher's property. Well over one year later, the conviction was reversed on appeal, and the district was forced to pay the teacher back-pay plus interest from the time the teacher was fired. Obviously, the legislation places school districts on the horns of a dilemma. They must either continue to employ teachers contrary to the statute, or face the risk of huge penalties if they immediately dismiss teachers convicted of felonies.

Conceptually, state legislatures should have repealed most of the statutory benefits for teachers who choose to bargain collectively; the existing dual system (contractual and statutory) of benefits for teachers really has no counterpart in the private sector. Granted, private-sector unions lobby for and sometimes achieve statutory benefits, but the differences are more than a matter of degree. Ironically, the outcome of teacher bargaining has been to increase the legislative demands of the teacher unions—precisely the opposite of what was anticipated when the teacher bargaining laws were enacted. Perhaps teachers should be required to choose statutory benefits without collective bargaining or collective bargaining without statutory benefits. The choice need not be quite so dichotomous, but the unrestricted pursuit of statutory benefits, similar if not identical to those achieved through collective bargaining, is undesirable public policy. In the private sector, the unions sometimes try to achieve by legislation what they cannot obtain through collective bargaining, but the practice is exceptional; in public education, it is an everyday occurrence. Of course, the teacher unions will not espouse the reform, but the practical question is the extent to which they will resist it.

The Anti-Profit Orientation of the Teacher Unions

Like other public employee organizations, the NEA and the AFT support higher taxes and a highly interventionist role for government at all levels. There is nothing remarkable about these positions, and much as one might disagree with them, they do not constitute an argument for a new union. One additional development, however, has led to a situation in which the economic philosophy of the teacher unions has adversely affected the classroom activities of teachers.

Like other unions, the NEA and the AFT oppose any measures that would pose a threat to union membership. In education, this opposition translates into opposition to "privatization," the union term for contracting out public services performed by union members. What is not so widely understood is that the teacher unions are engaged in an all-out effort to organize support personnel: school bus drivers, cafeteria workers, custodians, and so forth. The union appeal to these workers is that the union will protect them against "privatization," that is, against the possibility that school boards will contract with for-profit companies to provide the services currently provided by these employees.

The NEA and the AFT do not urge policymakers to consider the facts of each case to assess the desirability of privatization. Instead, the dynamics of union organizing have led the NEA and the AFT to demonize privatization per se. After all, the NEA and the AFT are not going to organize support staff by asserting that privatization issues must be resolved on a case-by-case basis. This common-sense position implies that privatization may be appropriate, an implication that does not appeal to support personnel who are afraid, usually for no good reason, that their jobs are in jeopardy.

In this context, the NEA/AFT fight against privatization requires a common denominator, and the common denominator turns out to be criticism of for-profit enterprise. To put it mildly, NEA/AFT publications and conventions are replete with denunciations of profits. These denunciations go far beyond criticisms of specific companies for specific actions. Profits are equated with greed, unscrupulous tactics, and callous indifference to the welfare of young children. At first glance, this incessant caricature of our economic system might be dismissed as merely another example of the tendency of interest groups to promote their interests by demonizing their opposition; in this case, however, the negative consequences of the tendency have profound implications for popular understanding of our economic system. Of course, market systems are not and should not be exempt from criticism, but the teacher union version of market systems is atrociously misleading in and out of classrooms. The new unionism that is needed on this issue need not advocate free markets, but at least it would avoid blatantly one-sided denunciations of them.

Occupational Citizenship

Many union issues are not resolved because we lack a concept of occupational citizenship. By "occupational citizenship," I refer to the relationships between individuals and their occupational organizations. The media and our educational system devote an endless stream of attention to elections for public office. Although union officials often play a more important role than public officials in the affairs of workers, virtually no attention is paid to union elections. Even when there is such attention, as in the 1997 contest for the presidency of the Teamsters union, virtually all of it is devoted to the personalities of the candidates; little or none is devoted to the basic issues of worker/union relationships.

In some respects, unions are anomalies in our social environment. They are private organizations, but government plays an indispensable role in forcing workers to join or pay service fees to them; there are few, if any, parallels to a situation in which government requires membership in a private organization, or compels individuals to contribute to it. Furthermore, union governance is largely a matter of government regulation, not of membership determination. Government has set the parameters, if not the details, of most aspects of union governance: how often elections are held, who may run for office, information to be made available to members, and so forth. The parameters are sometimes useful, but they illustrate the fact that "union democracy" is more dependent on government regulation than on membership control.

Quite often, government regulation of unions is an exercise in futility. For example, although federal regulations require private-sector unions to file reports showing the salaries paid to union officials, rank-and-file members cannot determine the total compensation of individual union officers and staff from the required government reports. This point is even more applicable to the teacher unions, most of which are not governed by federal reporting and disclosure requirements applicable to unions. And, to be blunt about it, the NEA and the AFT take the position that individual members do not have the right to know these closely guarded secrets. Any member who doubts this need only write to union officers for an item-by-item statement of union compensation per officer or staff member for retirement, insurance, leaves, holiday pay, severance pay, tuition reimbursement, and a host of other benefits too numerous to be listed here.

Parties who control the flow of information inevitably do so for their own welfare; teacher unions and their leaders are not an exception to this generalization. The new unionism that is needed may not remedy this problem completely or even adequately, but it will provide more useful information about the union than the NEA and the AFT currently provide. The union rebuttal is that disaffected members, for whatever reason, need only become more active in union affairs to achieve their objectives. This appears to be a "democratic" response to the problem of member dissatisfaction, but it is nothing of the sort. It relies on the fiction that dissatisfied members can devote their time and resources to union affairs, something that the overwhelming majority cannot do. The truly democratic solution would be to allow members to resign and/or cease contributing to the union at any time. This would ensure that members have a more feasible and more equal way to affect union policy. Granted, any such policy is likely to weaken the unions in their efforts to extract concessions from employers, but the new unionism needs to give strengthening the rights of individual members a higher priority than presenting a monolithic front to school employers.

Appendices*

A. Resolution New D-6, adopted by the 1997 Representative Assembly, National Education Association (NEA), July 5, 1997
B. Specific Goals for Interns and Consulting Teachers, Toledo School District
C. Teacher Summary Evaluation Report, Toledo School District
D. Four Year Contract Evaluation Form, Toledo School District
E. Principal Summary, Toledo School District

*The Columbus Education Association refused permission to publish the forms used in the Columbus peer review program. After asserting that the forms were the work of several entities, CEA President John Grossman asserted: "I cannot grant permission because I do not speak for the entire partnership, but only represent one of the entities." Actually, this declination is more significant than the forms, which are appendices to the agreement between the CEA and the Columbus Board of Education and are, therefore, in the public domain. The Columbus forms do not differ materially from those used in Toledo, but the declination illustrates the fear of critical review that pervades peer review districts.

Appendix A

Resolution New D,
*Peer Assistance and Review Programs**

(As adopted by the 1997 NEA Representative Assembly on July 5, 1997)

The National Education Association believes that high standards within the teaching profession and continuous improvement in professional practices are cornerstones of the profession. Some local associations may conclude that, under certain circumstances, a peer assistance or a peer assistance and review program is an appropriate mechanism for achieving these objectives.

The primary purpose of any such program should be to provide "assistance" (to improve professional practice, retain promising teachers, and build professional knowledge to improve student success). A local association may, as its option, also decide to include a "review" component in the program (involving the evaluation of performance). If a local association takes either position, the program should:

a. Be developed through collective bargaining or through a joint association/school district agreement in nonbargaining states.

b. Be governed by a board composed of an equal number or a majority of representatives appointed by the local association.

c. Acknowledge that the school district makes the final decision to retain or seek nonrenewal or termination, but that recommendations forwarded by the joint governing body are routinely accepted and acted upon by the district.

d. Ensure that only teachers who are deemed by their peers to be highly skilled practitioners are selected for the role of consulting teacher, that the consulting teacher's area of expertise is the same as or closely related to that of the participating teacher, and that the consulting teacher is chosen by the program governing bodies with the approval of the participating teacher involved.

---

*I have referred to this resolution elsewhere as "New D-6," the title it was given when it was originally submitted.

e. Seek consulting teachers who reflect the diverse population of the teaching staff.

f. Provide that consulting teachers are properly compensated and provided adequate time to fulfill their responsibilities.

g. Provide that consulting teachers receive extensive and ongoing training in mentoring/coaching skills, district initiatives and resources, and current education instructional methods.

h. Establish guidelines for the referral of teachers as well as safeguards to prevent unwarranted referrals.

i. Establish and convey to all consulting and participating teachers clear rules on allowable uses of documents, products, and communications arising from the program.

j. Require extensive documentation based on ongoing assessments of each participant.

k. Require that rigorous and extensive assistance be provided over an appropriate period of time to help the participating teacher attain the requisite standard of proficiency before any effort to counsel the participating teacher out of the profession is made or a recommendation to initiate nonrenewal or termination proceedings is issued.

l. Ensure due process protection and duty of fair representation procedures.

m. Guarantee that participating teachers, consulting teachers, and teachers who sit on governing bodies do not lose their Association membership or bargaining unit status by virtue of their participation in the program.

Appendix B

Specific Goals for Interns and Consulting Teachers

Definition of Terms

To promote uniformity of use, the following notes are to be used in interpreting the criteria of evaluation.

I. TEACHING PROCEDURES—PLANNING AND IMPLEMENTATION

A. *Skill in Planning*
1. Content and procedures are selected to achieve purposes of the lesson and of long-term plans.
2. Daily plans are written in the plan book detailed enough for the teacher's use or for a substitute, if necessary. (Where the plan book does not provide adequate space, teacher provides details on supplementary sheets of paper or cards.) These may be checked weekly by the principal, assistant principal, supervisor and/or intern consulting teacher.
3. There is thorough understanding of the material to be taught.
4. There is sufficient familiarity with the lesson plan and teacher's guides so that they are used effectively and creatively.
5. Plans provide variety, creativity and balance in the types of activities as well as transitions between activities and lessons.
6. Necessary chalk board preparation has been made prior to the beginning of the lesson. The chalk board should be used throughout the lesson for clarification as needed.

117

7. Teaching aids, such as cards, charts, books and films are ready for use.

B. *Assessment and Evaluation Skills*
1. The teacher's long-term planning includes periodic evaluation of the pupils' progress, both formal (e.g., quizzes, tests) and informal (e.g., non-verbal clues indicating whether the pupils comprehend the lesson).
2. The teacher also uses his or her judgment, based on such evaluations, in deciding when the material must be retaught because the pupils have not adequately grasped it.
3. The teacher will keep an up to date written record of student achievement to support evaluation.

C. *Skill in Making Assignments*
1. Pupils are helped to relate new subject matter to previous learnings.
2. Presentation follows planned steps for most effective learning and shows adjustment to needs of the group and individuals.
3. Worthwhile and interesting assignments are presented clearly, and explicit directions are given so that pupils know what is expected of them.
4. Class work and homework assignments are made realistic in length and level of difficulty according to the grade, ability and home background of the student.

D. *Skill in Developing Good Work-Study Habits*
1. High standards of work are consistently encouraged.
2. Opportunities are provided for creative, independent work.

E. *Resourceful Use of Instructional Materials*
1. A variety of material is used to stimulate interest and enrich learning.
2. Materials are properly related to the class work and are appropriately timed.
3. The teacher follows the authorized scope and sequence of instruction and provides the pupils with a variety of materials within the limitations of the resources made available.
4. The ideas of pupils and other approaches are considered although the Course of Study is the primary resource.

F. *Skill in Using Motivating Techniques*
1. The teacher uses questions leading into the day's work, pictures or other concrete materials, and short reviews.

2. Lessons provide a balance of pupil and teacher interaction.
3. The enthusiasm of the teacher is sustained throughout the lesson.

G. *Skill in Questioning Techniques*
   Questions . . .
   1. Are closely related to pupils' level of comprehension and appropriate to the purpose, subject area and class (e.g., closed versus open-ended).
   2. Make pupils think reflectively and deeply.
   3. Motivate them to read, to find out, and to create.
   4. Help pupils clarify meanings and check understandings.
   5. Help pupils organize their thinking in a logical way.
   6. Help pupils pull a number of ideas together, generalize.
   7. Point out how new learnings can be applied.
   8. Offer positive confirmation of pupils' responses (paraphrasing, etc.).

H. *Ability to Recognize and Provide for Individual Differences*
   1. The teacher shows a personal interest in each pupil's progress whether or not individualized techniques are used.
   2. Individual pupils are helped to achieve the maximum of their abilities through the teacher's use of a variety of assignments and teaching methods with the class.

I. *Oral and Written Communications Skills*
   1. The teacher demonstrates the ability to communicate effectively in both oral and written expression.
   2. Command of Standard English is demonstrated through correct syntax and grammar.
   3. The teacher does not exhibit any language patterns which would inhibit effective communication to the students.

J. *Speech, Articulation and Voice Quality*
   1. The quality and control of the teacher's voice does not present an obstacle to learning. (For example, in the primary grades, the teacher's distinct enunciation of different vowel sounds is necessary to teach reading; a teacher's voice that is too low to be heard will hinder instruction.)
   2. This is not intended to exclude individuals with speech impediments or problems from teaching. However, if the teacher's voice or articulation actually interferes with pupil learning, the teacher must do whatever is necessary and possible to correct the problem.

II. CLASSROOM MANAGEMENT

A. *Effective Classroom Facilitation and Control*
  1. The teacher sets up and maintains reasonable rules of conduct.
  2. The teacher provides conscious modeling to modify attitudes and behaviors.
  3. Pupil growth in self-discipline and a positive self-concept are encouraged.

B. *Effective Interaction with Pupils*
  1. The consistent practice of fairness in teacher-pupil relationships is apparent.
  2. There is evidence of understanding and respect for pupils as individuals.
  3. The teacher provides opportunities for self-expression and self-determination and deals with both the cognitive and affective.

C. *Efficient Classroom Routine*
  1. The teacher effectively carries out daily routines and administrative requests.
  2. Observation indicates good storage and distribution of educational supplies and materials. Also the physical arrangement of furniture and the pattern of the teacher's movement within the room enhance the learning process.

D. *Confidence/Stability*
  1. Projects confidence in his/her teaching ability.
  2. Exhibits physical vigor and enthusiasm.
  3. Exhibits consistent disposition and appropriate behavior toward students even during an unforeseen incident or interruption.
  4. Demonstrates emotional self-control.

E. *Reasonable, Fair and Impartial in Dealing With Students*
  1. Recognizes his/her proper role.
  2. Makes students aware of his/her expectations.
  3. Does not demonstrate individual or group bias.

III. KNOWLEDGE OF SUBJECT—ACADEMIC PREPARATION

A. The teacher demonstrates knowledge of subject through classroom performance and academic records.

B. The teacher demonstrates academic preparation to teach the subjects assigned.

IV. PERSONAL CHARACTERISTICS AND PROFESSIONAL
RESPONSIBILITY

A. *Genuine Interest in Teaching*
1. Exhibits a positive, professional attitude toward teaching.
2. Demonstrates respect and consideration for pupils as individuals.
3. Is receptive to innovative educational concepts.

B. *Personal Appearance*
1. Exhibits good personal hygiene and neatness.
2. Presents an appearance that does not adversely affect the students' ability to learn.

C. *Skill in Adapting to Change*
The teacher is able to adapt the lesson even when unexpectedly interrupted.

D. *Acceptance of Policies and Procedures of the Toledo Public Schools*
Acceptance of written policies and procedures of the Toledo Public Schools is expected.

E. *Responsible Both Inside and Outside the Classroom*
1. Appropriately monitors class.
2. Attends required after-school activities and meetings.

F. *Cooperative Approach Toward Parents and School Personnel*

G. *Punctual and Regular in Attendance*

Appendix C

Teacher Summary Evaluation Report, Toledo School District

TEACHER SUMMARY EVALUATION REPORT

Name _____

College _____

School _____ Date _____

Grade or

Subject _____

| Period of Sept.-Dec. ☐ | Period of Jan.-March ☐ | Period of Apr.-Dec. ☐ |

Certification _____

Number of Observations and Time _____ Conference Time _____

Intern semesters completed _____

Check on March and Dec. Report	Check on March Report Only	Contract Status
☐ Outstanding	☐ Recommended for first one-year contract	☐ First year contract
☐ Satisfactory		☐ Second year contract
☐ Unsatisfactory	☑ Recommended for second one-year contract	☐ Four-year contract
☐ Written comment only	☐ Recommended for initial four-year contract	☐ One-year contract
☐ Irregular Term		☐ Continuing contract
☐ Recommended for 2nd semester intern program	☐ Recommended for third one-year contract	☐ Long-term substitute (60 or more days)
	☐ Not recommended for reappointment	

*OUTSTANDING: Performance shows exceptional professional qualities and growth.

SATISFACTORY: Performance at expected and desired professional qualities and growth.

*UNSATISFACTORY: Performance shows serious weaknesses or deficiencies.

*For more complete definition refer to page 10 in The Toledo Plan.

*Unsatisfactories and/or outstandings must have a written supportive statement.

	Out-standing	Satis-factory	Unsatis-factory
I. TEACHING PROCEDURES			
A. Skill in planning			
B. Skill in assessment and evaluation			
C. Skill in making assignments			
D. Skill in developing good work-study habits			
E. Resourceful use of instructional materials			
F. Skill in using motivating techniques			
G. Skill in questioning techniques			
H. Ability to recognize and provide for individual differences			
I. Oral and written communication skills			
J. Speech, articulation and voice quality			
II. CLASSROOM MANAGEMENT			
A. Effective classroom facilitation and control			
B. Effective interaction with pupils			
C. Efficient classroom routine			
D. Confidence/stability			
E. Is reasonable, fair and impartial in dealing with students			
III. KNOWLEDGE OF SUBJECT — ACADEMIC PREPARATION			
IV. PERSONAL CHARACTERISTICS AND PROFESSIONAL RESPONSIBILITY			
A. Shows a genuine interest in teaching			
B. Personal appearance			
C. Skill in adapting to change			
D. Adheres to accepted policies and procedures of Toledo Public Schools			
E. Accepts responsibility both inside and outside the classroom			
F. Has a cooperative approach toward parents and school personnel			
G. Is punctual and regular in attendance			

Evaluator's Signature (when required) _____

Teacher's Signature _____

Principal's Signature (when required) _____

Evaluator's Position _____

Date of Conference _____

DIRECTIONS

1. Rate all categories, bold face and subcategories.
2. Attach all supporting documents that have been signed or initiated.

Appendix D

*Four Year Contract Evaluation Form**

*The Four Year Contract Evaluation Form serves as the Teacher Intervention Form in the Toledo School District.

FOUR YEAR CONTRACT EVALUATION FORM*

Toledo School District

All teachers serving in their fourth year of a four year limited contract will be evaluated. A copy of the completed evaluation form must be on file in the Office of Human Resources, Room 102 on or before March 20. The following teacher is employed under a limited contract which expires in June.

Name _____   School _____

Grade/Subject _____   Date _____

I. **Teaching Techniques**
Includes planning and organizing; skill in presenting subject; ability to motivate; recognition of individual differences; and ability to develop good work habits and attitudes, etc.

High   Low

II. **Classroom Control**
Includes rapport with pupils; respect for rules; atmosphere for learning; and efficient routines, etc.

High   Low

III. **Knowledge of Subject**

High   Low

IV. **Personal Characteristics**
Includes responsibility, dependability, interest, enthusiasm, effective speech, personal appearance, health and emotional stability.

High   Low

(IF NECESSARY, USE REVERSE SIDE FOR ADDITIONAL COMMENTS)

RECOMMENDED FOR A FOUR YEAR CONTRACT   YES_____   NO_____

_____   _____
(Teacher's signature)   (Principal's signature)

Copy to: Executive Director
          School Office
          Teacher
          Office of Human Resources

*If a tenured teacher receives an unsatisfactory rating, the Intern Board of Review may assign a consulting teacher or another peer to observe and evaluate the teacher. The second evaluation is given equal weight with the first. If both are "unsatisfactory," the Intern Board of Review can assign a one year contract in the intervention program in lieu of dismissal proceedings.

Appendix E

Principal Summary,
Toledo School District

PRINCIPAL SUMMARY

Date Sent _____

Teacher _____ To Be Returned By _____

School _____ Principal _____ Date Returned _____

Conference with Consultant Requested_____

Grade or subject _____
Period of Sept-Dec ☐
Period of Jan-Mar ☐
Period of April-June ☐
Other _____

| SATISFACTORY: Performance shows expected and desired professional qualities and growth. |
| *UNSATISFACTORY: Performance shows serious weakness and deficiencies. |
| *For more complete definition, refer to page 10 in The Toledo Plan. |
| *Unsatisfactories must have a written supportive statement. |

I. ABSENCE: Illness _____ Professional _____ Personal _____ Late Arrival _____

   a. Number of days in assignment: _____

	Satisfactory	Unsatisfactory
II. ADHERENCE TO:		
a. written district policy		
b. building policy		
c. district discipline policy		

III. PUNCTUALITY WITH REPORTS		

IV. COOPERATION WITH PARENTS		

V. COOPERATION WITH OTHER SCHOOL PERSONNEL		

COMMENTS FOR ITEMS I. TO V. OR OTHER DOCUMENTED INFORMATION

_____

_____

_____

_____

_____
Principal's Signature

_____
Teacher's Signature

_____ _____
Consulting Teacher's Signature   Date

Notes

Chapter 1. Introduction: Why This Book?

1. National Commission on Excellence in Education, *A Nation at Risk: The Imperative for Educational Reform* (Washington, DC: National Commission on Excellence in Education, 1983).
2. "Statement of Robert F. Chase," National Press Club, February 11, 1998.
3. In order to present Chase's version of the "new unionism" without any changes, I requested permission from Chase to publish his news release relating to this speech verbatim as an appendix to this book. Neither Chase nor anyone else at the NEA responded to my request.
4. Robert F. Chase, "The New NEA," address to the National Press Club, February 5, 1997. See also "Working USA Interview: Bob Chase, NEA President," *Working USA* (July/August 1997), p. 55.
5. *An Institution at Risk: An External Communications Review of the National Education Association,* submitted by the Kamber Group, January 17, 1997. The review is widely referred to as "The Kamber Report."
6. Charles C. Heckscher, *The New Unionism* (Ithaca, NY: Cornell University Press, 1996).

Chapter 2. Peer Review in Operation

1. Information about the Toledo peer review program was obtained in several face-to-face meetings with Dal Lawrence, president of the Toledo Federation of Teachers (TFT) from 1969 to 1997, with Jane Steger, consulting teacher, 1990–93, and from several documents provided by Lawrence. Among the latter, the most useful were

129

Intern Intervention Evaluation, a joint publication of the Toledo School District and the Toledo Federation of Teachers (May 1996), and "Teacher Excellence: Teachers Take Charge," *American Educator* (Spring 1984), pp. 22–29. Information about the Columbus program was obtained in a meeting with Columbus Education Association (CEA) president John Grossman, from the contract between the CEA and the Columbus school district, and from supplementary documents provided by Grossman.

2. Interview with former TFT president Dal Lawrence in Toledo, August 7, 1997.
3. *Ibid.*
4. See *Intern Intervention Evaluation,* p. 2. Italics in original.
5. Source: Surveys of consulting teachers, Toledo Federation of Teachers.
6. Source: Toledo Federation of Teachers.
7. Source: Columbus Education Association.
8. Source: Columbus Education Association.

Chapter 3. Principals under Peer Review

1. Ohio Revised Code, 4117.01(F).
2. National Labor Relations Act (1947), Section 14A.
3. Ohio Revised Code, 4117.09(D).
4. Dal Lawrence in "Teacher Excellence: Teachers Take Charge," *American Educator,* Spring 1984, p. 26.
5. Bill Harshberger, "Should NEA Affiliates Help Get Rid of Bad Teachers?" *NEA Today,* November 1987, p. 43.
6. Superintendent Merrill Grant, "Grant: School District's Proposals Reasonable," *Toledo Blade,* November 25, 1997, p. 11.

Chapter 5. Due Process and the Duty of Fair Representation under Peer Review

1. Ohio Revised Code, 4117.09(D). See discussion in Chapter 3.
2. Brief submitted by the Toledo Federation of Teachers, in the matter of fact finding between the Toledo Federation of Teachers, AFL-CIO, and the Toledo Board of Education, SERB Case No. 97-MED-07-0741.
3. Information provided by Toledo Public Schools.

Chapter 6. The Costs of Peer Review

1. Arthur E. Wise, Linda Darling-Hammond, Milbrey W. McLaughlin, and Harriet T. Bernstein, *Teacher Evaluation: A Study of Effective Practices* (Santa Monica, CA: Rand, June 1984), p. 37.

2. For example, see Lisa Birk, "Intervention: A Few Teachers' Unions Take the Lead in Policing Their Own," *Harvard Education Letter,* vol. 10, no. 6 (November/December 1994).
3. Grossman asserted to the author that the administrator time devoted to the program was "donated," which is probably news to the administrators involved.

Chapter 7. Peer Review in Other Contexts

1. Memorandum of Agreement between Saturn Corporation (Saturn), a wholly-owned subsidiary of General Motors Corporation (GM) and the International Union, United Automobile, Aerospace and Agricultural Implement Workers of America (Union) (1994). Italics added. The letter from Yokich to LeFauve is included in the Memorandum of Agreement, p. 25.
2. Source: Agreement between the Columbus Board of Education and the Columbus Education Association, effective until June 30, 2000.
3. Steve Lemken, "Editor's Corner," *NEA Today,* November 1997, p. 1.
4. Interview with Dal Lawrence, August 7, 1997.
5. *NLRB v. Yeshiva University,* 444 U.S. 672 (1980).
6. See Myron Lieberman, "Faculty Self Government: The Triumph of the Academic Mystique," *Government Union Review,* Spring 1985, pp. 40–54.

Chapter 8. The Union Stake in Peer Review

1. Robert C. Long and R. Theodore Clark, Jr., *Evaluation of the Collective Bargaining Agreements of the Toledo Public Schools* (Toledo, OH: Toledo Chamber of Commerce Community Coalition for Effective Education, September 30, 1995).
2. *Ibid.*
3. Christine E. Murray, Gerald Grant, and Raji Swaminathan, "Rochester's Reforms: The Right Prescription?" *Phi Delta Kappan,* October 1997, pp. 148–55.

Chapter 9. Peer Review: Summary and Conclusions

1. TFT submission to fact finder Mitchell Goldberg, November 24, 1997.
2. Arthur E. Wise, Linda Darling-Hammond, Milbrey W. McLaughlin, and Harriet T. Bernstein, *Teacher Evaluation: A Study of Effective Practices* (Santa Monica, CA: Rand, 1984).
3. Charles T. Kerchner, Julia E. Koppich, and Joseph G. Weeres, *United Mind Workers* (San Francisco: Jossey-Bass, 1996), p. 44.
4. National Commission on Teaching and America's Future, *What Matters Most: Teaching for America's Future* (New York: Teachers College, Columbia University, 1996), p. 56.

5. "Should NEA Affiliates Help Get Rid of Bad Teachers?" *NEA Today Online,* November 1997, p. 4. The NEA closed the voting and its Interactive Forum on December 20, 1997.
6. The Columbus Education Association is developing model peer review plans for districts of different sizes. For various reasons, these models were not reviewed in conducting this study.
7. "Toledo School District Achieves Better 9th Grade Exam Results," *Toledo Blade,* November 1, 1997, p. 9.
8. "Peer Assistance and Review with John Grossman," *NEA Today Online,* November 19, 1997.
9. In a presentation at the National Press Club on February 11, 1998, NEA president Robert Chase emphasized the NEA's determination to promote peer review.
10. For a striking example of favorable media treatment of the new unionism that does not raise any hard questions about it, see "A Different Kind of Union," *Education Week,* October 29, 1997, pp. 1, 26–31.

Chapter 10. Beyond Peer Review: The New Unionism That Is Needed

1. Unless otherwise noted, sources for the factual statements in this chapter may be found in Myron Lieberman, *The Teacher Unions* (New York: Free Press, 1997).
2. See *ibid.,* pp. 245–64, for a discussion of some of these options.

Index

About the Author

Myron Lieberman is a Senior Research Scholar of the Social Philosophy and Policy Center. He was educated at the University of Minnesota and the University of Illinois and has taught at the University of Pennsylvania, Ohio University, the University of Southern California, and the City University of New York. He has served as a consultant to six state legislative bodies and several national organizations on questions of collective bargaining, as an expert witness, and as a chief negotiator or consultant in collective bargaining in numerous school districts.

Dr. Lieberman is the author of fifteen books on education policy, including *Privatization and Educational Choice* (1989), *Public Education: An Autopsy* (1993), and *The Teacher Unions* (1997).

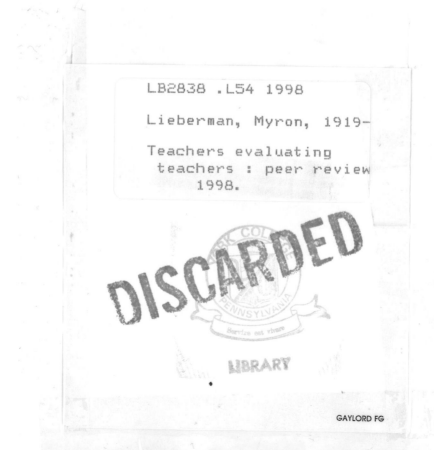